TOM

PROBLEMS OF DEATH

Opposing Viewpoints

PROBLEMS OF DEATH

Opposing Viewpoints

David L. Bender

OPPOSING VIEWPOINTS SERIES

SECOND EDITION

Greenhaven Press
577 Shoreview Park Road
St. Paul, Minnesota 55126

Library of Congress Cataloging in Publication Data
Main entry under title:

Problems of death.

(Opposing viewpoints series)
Bibliography: p.
Summary: Presents opposing viewpoints on euthanasia, abortion, suicide, and funeral homes through essays by a variety of authors. Includes discussion activities.
1. Death—Moral and ethical aspects—Addresses, essays, lectures. 2. Undertakers and undertaking—Addresses, essays, lectures.
[1. Euthanasia—Addresses, essays, lectures. 2. Abortion—Addresses, essays, lectures. 3. Suicide—Addresses, essays, lectures. 4. Undertakers and undertaking—Addresses, essays, lectures] I. Bender, David L., 1936-   . II. Series.
HQ1073.P76 1985   306'.9   85-8070
ISBN 0-89908-335-8 (lib. bdg.)
ISBN 0-89908-310-2 (pbk.)

CONGRESS SHALL MAKE NO LAW... ABRIDGING THE FREEDOM OF SPEECH, OR OF THE PRESS

first amendment to the U.S. Constitution

The basic foundation of our democracy is the first amendment guarantee of freedom of expression. The OPPOSING VIEW-POINTS SERIES is dedicated to the concept of this basic freedom and the idea that it is more important to practice it than to enshrine it.

TABLE OF CONTENTS

the Opposing viewpoints series

THE IMPORTANCE OF EXAMINING
OPPOSING VIEWPOINTS

The purpose of this book, and the Opposing Viewpoints Series as a whole, is to confront you with alternative points of view on complex and sensitive issues.

Perhaps the best way to inform yourself is to analyze the positions of those who are regarded as experts and well studied on the issues. It is important to consider every variety of opinion in an attempt to determine the truth. Opinions from the mainstream of society should be examined. Also important are opinions that are considered radical, reactionary, minority or stigmatized by some other uncomplimentary label. An important lesson of history is the fact that many unpopular and even despised opinions eventually gained widespread acceptance. The opinions of Socrates, Jesus and Galileo are good examples of this.

You will approach this book with opinions of your own on the issues debated within it. To have a good grasp of your own viewpoint you must understand the arguments of those with whom you disagree. It is said that those who do not completely understand their adversary's point of view do not fully understand their own.

Perhaps the most persuasive case for considering opposing viewpoints has been presented by John Stuart Mill in his work *On Liberty*. Consider the following statements of his when studying controversial issues.

THE OPINIONS OF OTHERS

If all mankind minus one were of one opinion, and only one person were of the contrary opinion, mankind would be no more justified in silencing that one person than he, if he had the power, would be justified in silencing mankind....

We can never be sure that the opinion we are endeavoring to stifle is a false opinion...

All silencing of discussion is an assumption of infallibility....

Ages are no more infallible than individuals; every age having held many opinions which subsequent ages have deemed not only false but absurd; and it is as certain that many opinions now general will be rejected by future ages....

The only way in which a human being can make some approach to knowing the whole of a subject, is by hearing what can be said about it by persons of every variety of opinion, and studying all modes in which it can be looked at by every character of mind. No wise man ever acquired his wisdom in any mode but this....

The beliefs which we have most warrant for have no safeguard to rest on but a standing invitation to the whole world to prove them unfounded....

To call any proposition certain, while there is any one who would deny its certainty if permitted, but who is not permitted, is to assume that we ourselves and those who agree with us are the judges of certainty, and judges without hearing the other side....

Men are not more zealous for truth than they are for error, and a sufficient application of legal or even social penalties will generally succeed in stopping the propagation of either....

However unwilling a person who has a strong opinion may admit the possibility that his opinion may be false, he ought to be moved by the consideration that, however true it may be, if it is not fully, frequently, and fearlessly discussed, it will be a dead dogma, not a living truth.

From *On Liberty* by John Stuart Mill.

A pitfall to avoid in considering alternative points of view is that of regarding your own point of view as being merely common sense and the most rational stance, and the point of view of others as being only opinion and naturally wrong. It may be that the opinion of others is correct and that yours is in error.

Another pitfall to avoid is that of closing your mind to the opinions of those whose views differ from yours. The best way to approach a dialogue is to make your primary purpose that of understanding the mind and arguments of the other person and not that of enlightening him or her with your solutions. One learns more by listening than by speaking.

It is my hope that after reading this book you will have a deeper understanding of the issues debated and will appreciate the complexity of even seemingly simple issues when good and honest people disagree. This awareness is particularly important in a democratic society such as ours, where people enter into public debate to determine the common good. People with whom you disagree should not be regarded as enemies, but rather as friends who suggest a different path to a common goal.

ANALYZING SOURCES OF INFORMATION

The Opposing Viewpoints Series uses diverse sources; magazines, journals, books, newspapers, statements and position papers from a wide range of individuals and organizations. These sources help in the development of a mindset that is open to the consideration of a variety of opinions.

The format of the Opposing Viewpoints Series should help you answer the following questions.

1. *Are you aware that three of the most popular weekly news magazines, Time, Newsweek, and U.S. News and World Report are not totally objective accounts of the news?*
2. **Do you know there is no such thing as a completely objective author, book, newspaper or magazine?**
3. **Do you think that because a magazine or newspaper article is unsigned it is always a statement of facts rather than opinions?**
4. **How can you determine the point of view of newspapers and magazines?**
5. **When you read do you question an author's frame of reference (political persuasion, training, and life experience)?**

Many people finish their formal education unable to cope with these basic questions. They have little chance to understand the social forces and issues surrounding them. Some fall easy victims to demagogues preaching solutions to problems by scapegoating minorities with conspiratorial and paranoid explanations of complex social issues.

I do not want to imply that anything is wrong with authors and publications that have a political slant or bias. All authors have a frame of reference. Readers should understand this. You should also understand that almost all writers have a point of view. An important skill in reading is to be able to locate and identify a point of view. This series gives you practice in both.

DEVELOPING BASIC THINKING SKILLS

A number of basic skills for critical thinking are practiced in the discussion activities that appear throughout the books in the series. Some of the skills are:

Locating a Point of View The ability to determine which side of an issue an author supports.

Evaluating Sources of Information The ability to choose from among alternative sources the most reliable and accurate source in relation to a given subject.

Distinguishing Between Primary and Secondary Sources The ability to understand the important distinction between sources which are primary (original or eyewitness accounts) and those which are secondary (historically removed from, and based on, primary sources).

Separating Fact from Opinion The ability to make the basic distinction between factual statements (those which can be demonstrated or verified empirically) and statements of opinion (those which are beliefs or attitudes that cannot be proved).

Distinguishing Between Prejudice and Reason The ability to differentiate between statements of prejudice (unfavorable, preconceived judgments based on feelings instead of reason) and statements of reason (conclusions that can be clearly and logically explained or justified).

Identifying Stereotypes The ability to identify oversimplified, exaggerated descriptions (favorable or unfavorable) about people and insulting statements about racial, religious or national groups, based upon misinformation or lack of information.

Recognizing Ethnocentrism The ability to recognize attitudes or opinions that express the view that one's own race, culture, or group is inherently superior, or those attitudes that judge another race, culture, or group in terms of one's own.

It is important to consider opposing viewpoints. It is equally important to be able to critically analyze those viewpoints. The discussion activities in this book will give you practice in mastering these thinking skills.

Using this book, and others in the series, will help you develop critical thinking skills. These skills should improve your ability to better understand what you read. You should be better able to separate fact from opinion, reason from rhetoric. You should become a better consumer of information in our media-centered culture.

A VALUES ORIENTATION

Throughout the Opposing Viewpoints Series you are presented conflicting values. A good example is *American Foreign Policy*. The first chapter debates whether foreign policy should be based on the same kind of moral principles that individuals use in guiding their personal actions, or instead be based primarily on doing what best advances national interests, regardless of moral implications.

The series does not advocate a particular set of values. Quite the contrary! The very nature of the series leaves it to you, the reader, to formulate the values orientation that you find most suitable. My purpose, as editor of the series, is to see that this is made possible by offering a wide range of viewpoints which are fairly presented.

David L. Bender
Opposing Viewpoints Series Editor

DEATH: THE GREAT EQUALIZER

"Death comes equally to us all, and makes us all equal when it comes."
John Donne, *Sermons*

When the first edition of *Problems of Death* was published in 1974, it dealt with, among other topics, the questions of suicide, abortion and euthanasia. In that year, there were 25,683 reported suicides and 763,476 legal abortions in the United States. By 1980, the number of suicides and abortions had risen to over 28,000 and 1,200,000 respectively. Regarding euthanasia, in 1974, the moral and legal implications of "mercy killing" were just beginning to be debated on a national scale by physicians, clergymen and legislators. Yet two years later, 38 state legislatures were considering right-to-die or euthanasia bills with California's Natural Death Act being the first of those bills to become law on January 1, 1977.

The timeliness of the first *Problems of Death* book and of this present revision is evidenced by the statistics quoted above. The number of suicides and abortions has increased dramatically in less than a decade. Passive euthanasia, or the withdrawal of life sustaining devices such as respirators from terminally ill patients, is being employed with growing frequency. On the other hand, opponents of abortion and euthanasia are becoming more vocal and adament in their demands that legislation be passed outlawing these practices.

The second edition of *Problems of Death* contains viewpoints which reflect recent and anticipated statistical trends and socio-religious attitudes. Other viewpoints offer arguments which are, in the editor's opinion, timeless and not subject to changing mores.

Of the numerous changes and additions to the second edition, two deserve explanation. Chapter three in the first edition, which debated the pros and cons of capital punishment, has been removed and a revised version has been included in the newly published series title, *Criminal Justice: Opposing Viewpoints*. Inasmuch as suicide, abortion and euthanasia are elective issues and capital punishment is not, it was decided that the latter should be excluded. The second change is in the chapter on suicide. The number of viewpoints in that chapter has been increased from two to six. The alarming increase in the rate of suicide coupled with a growing agreement among many human services professionals that suicide or "auto-euthanasia" should be a matter of personal choice, underlined the need for a broader spectrum of viewpoints.

Finally, the reader should be aware that because the issues dealt with in this anthology are highly sensitive, the editor has attempted to employ a comparable sensitivity by striving for fairness and balance in the selection of both viewpoints and visuals. The debate on the issues presented will undoubtedly continue for many years. It is therefore the editor's hope that after reading this anthology, the reader will be able to participate in these debates from a wider and more informed perspective.

Chapter 1

PROBLEMS OF DEATH

Should Euthanasia Be Allowed?

"I favor merciful termination of life; no discussion necessary... I favor owning one's own life."

I Favor Merciful Termination of Life

Stewart V. Pahl

Stewart V. Pahl has studied euthanasia or "good death" since 1971 and has written and lectured extensively on the subject. A member of the American Humanist Association and the National Writers Club, he was a Humanist Counselor when this viewpoint was originally published. In it, Mr. Pahl recommends that limited and safeguarded euthanasia be employed as a decent and merciful way to eliminate the unnecessary suffering of prolonged dying.

Consider the following questions while reading:

1. **What does the author mean by the statement "I favor mercy"?**
2. **What safeguard does the author recommend to insure that the practice of euthanasia is not abused?**
3. **How does he react to the possibility that the practice of euthanasia will be abused and used improperly?**

Stewart V. Pahl, "I Favor Mercy," **The Humanist**, September/October, 1972. Reprinted by permission.

Everyone terminates life prematurely. Even vegetarians terminate the lives of plants, and step on a worm occasionally. When we discuss this issue, the major considerations, therefore have to do with degree, manner, and intent; there is no question as to "whether," since we all terminate life for other entities. The main questions are: much or little, cruel or merciful, intentional or unintentional.

Nature itself terminates most lives long before their longevity expectancy. Millions of sperm die for each one that lives. Further, the number of human lives terminated by "natural causes" far exceeds the number of those ending when a person simply does not awaken some morning after he has reached the age of 100 or 120.

MERCIFUL TERMINATION OF LIFE

I favor merciful termination of life; no discussion necessary. I favor intentional termination of life, since most of us engage in such action without giving it much thought. I favor owning one's own life.

Some time ago, it was almost unheard of that a person could own his own body. Next of kin owned the body after death. Now, in many states, a person can will his body to a medical school, for example, and such a pre-death statement of intent is binding upon next of kin. Some day, the law will shift so that individuals will own their own lives as well as their own bodies.

Obviously, this will make suicide legal. I regret this somewhat, but not to the point of being greatly disturbed. The greater good derives from the possibility of legalizing euthanasia for those who want it. Safeguarded euthanasia would eliminate most of the necessity of caring for "vegetables," a necessity that now preempts manpower that should be devoted to the living, not to the dying and the already "dead." It would eliminate such unnecessary suffering; it would make a satisfying departure possible in many instances where a degrading, repulsive death is now the only legal possibility.

PRECAUTIONS FOR LEGAL EUTHANASIA

It would be easy to include safeguards, so that a few euthanasianists could not arbitrarily do away with all rich kinfolk for the sake of money-hungry inheritors. Reasonable precautions might include such provisions as these:

1. The state could stipulate the number of individuals who should agree when euthanasia might be practiced. This could be, for example, three persons: two M.D.'s and one nearest of kin.

2. The state could stipulate how frequently an individual, or group of individuals, may be permitted to sign a euthanasia authorization. The rule might be: "No two persons shall sign a euthanasia authorization oftener than twice a year." This safeguard would prevent two or three "professional euthanasianists" from habitually signing authorizations — for a fee, of course, depending upon how much the beneficiaries were to inherit.

INCREASED INTEREST IN EUTHANASIA

Physicians in a modern hospital appear to have no capacity to stop their therapeutic enthusiasm, or to temper their drive to do whatever they are capable of doing with any consideration of the patient's feelings and wishes. This has led people to seek ways of controlling what might happen to them under similar circumstances. This increased public interest has made itself evident in support for legislation to allow voluntary euthanasia and in the popularity of signed statements of one's wishes such as the "Living Will."

Michael A. Simpson, *The Facts of Death*, 1979.

3. The state might well stipulate that no euthanasia could be authorized except when so directed by the individual himself (generally on a prior basis, when in good health and sound mind). Rare exceptions would be made in some cases, when a person had for some time been legally incompetent and medically incurable.

It will be said that there will be abuses; this is true. I know of no custom, however good, that does not have its abuses. It is said that practicing some euthanasia will make it progressively acceptable to do away with everybody who becomes

"The artificial life support systems are intact, but I'd say Mr. Phipps could use a talking to."

a slight nuisance to anybody else. This is absurd. The state has engaged in legalized termination of life for many centuries, and never yet has this practice become so out of hand as to deplete the population beyond recovery. When abuses increase unbearably, the people revise the statutes. No laws or customs are perfect.

For our own time, and for a generation or two, I think it would be on the side of decency and mercy to permit (the law doesn't have to do more than permit) limited, safeguarded euthanasia. No amount of sentimentalizing can hide the fact that hundreds, even thousands, of elderly persons would cheerfully kiss the world farewell if only they were permitted to do this legally and gracefully. Among the living, some would applaud this decision selfishly and some would applaud unselfishly.

SENTIMENTALITY AND CRUELTY

Traditionally, we have been both sentimental and cruel in dealing with human lives. We've been sentimental when a

21

child has fallen into a well, for example, and we have commanded incalculable manpower and material to rescue the child. But if someone had suggested previously that we spend $3.27 in order to cover the abandoned well satisfactorily so that a child couldn't fall into it, we would have turned away and shrugged, cruelly, indifferently. In general, that's the way we have too often dealt with life and death.

In early American days, as now, no physician would have dared to practice euthanasia. Yet the sentimental state that forbade this merciful custom of euthanasia was the selfsame cruel state that legalized slavery. We have a long inherited history of cruelty and sentimentality flourishing side by side in our customs, our laws, our attitudes.

I propose mercy. I place human wellbeing at the top of my list of priorities. I am willing to redefine "life" and "death" for the sake of such human well-being. When "life" is gone, let us govern ourselves accordingly and be decent toward the "remains."

"The new ethic tells us that certain kinds of people in certain circumstances, are worth more dead than alive."

Euthanasia Should Not Be Permitted

John M. Hendrickson and Thomas St. Martin

Thomas St. Martin is past president of Minnesota Citizens Concerned for Life and currently is a community faculty member in Public Administration at Metropolitan State University, St. Paul, Minnesota. He co-authored the following viewpoint with Dr. John M. Hendrickson, a radiologist and past member of the board of directors of Minnesota Citizens Concerned for Life. In it, the authors argue that "positive" euthanasia is a philosophy which the medical profession and our democratic society must never accept.

Consider the following questions while reading:
1. **What is meant by the term *new ethic*?**
2. **What do the authors claim is the basic fallacy of the euthanasia argument?**
3. **What is the distinction between *positive* euthanasia and *negative* euthanasia?**

John M. Hendrickson and Thomas St. Martin, "Euthanasia and the 'New Ethic'," **The Wanderer,** August 16, 1973. Reprinted with permission from **The Wanderer.**

We have been propelled into the abortion era by a new ethic which places relative value on human life; the same ethic has now brought us to the threshold of the euthanasia era. The notion that each and every human life (regardless of condition or social "usefulness") is inviolable has been eroded. It is being rapidly replaced by a philosophy of over-practical realism—by a philosophy which understands "rightness" and "goodness" in terms of "usefulness". Life is no longer an absolute "good" in and of itself; the taking of life is justified in the interests of ensuring the greatest good for the greatest number. Thus, the relatively "useless" lives of the pre-natal human being or the aged human being can be destroyed in the interests of some greater social "benefit." In effect, the new ethic tells us that certain kinds of people in certain circumstances, are worth more dead than alive.

FALLACY OF EUTHANASIA ARGUMENT

The basic fallacy of the euthanasia argument is this belief that life is expendable (under certain conditions), and worse, that some men are able to discern when another man's life falls into that category. It is the result of a falsification of life that our Madison Avenue society has created; that unless we are youthful, beautiful, intelligent and physically whole our lives cannot be fully worthwhile or "useful." We must reject this vicious doctrine and realize that the gift of life itself is the basis for everything else.

EUTHANASIA IS STILL MURDER

"Euthanasia" is defined as "the putting of a person to death painlessly." That is not euthanasia; it is homicide. If you "put a person to death," that is, deliberately kill him, you are committing murder. If it is done painlessly, it is still murder.

Fredric Wertham, *Death, Dying and Euthanasia,* Dennis J. Horan and David Mall, eds.

But what is euthanasia? Strictly defined, it means "good death." According to the dictionary it means "...inducing the painless death of a person for reasons assumed to be merci-

24

'The pedestal's not what it used to be'

ful." A common synonym is "mercy killing."

Anyone who has seen a close relative or friend dying from a hopelessly incurable and unbearably painful illness (such as terminal cancer) feels the weight of the argument that the "humane" thing to do is to painlessly help the suffering patient out of his misery. Herein lies the superficial appeal of the pro-euthanasia argument.

This does not mean that a hopelessly ill patient must be kept alive by any and every means available. Everyone accepts the principle that the use of extraordinary means is not required in every case.

POSITIVE AND NEGATIVE EUTHANASIA

Our real concern must be with what is often termed "positive" euthanasia as distinct from "negative" euthanasia—the withholding of life sustaining measures from a hopelessly ill or dying patient). The concept of positive euthanasia centers on the distinction between causing death to occur and permitting death to occur; a distinction between active and passive behavior.

To actively terminate a human life for whatever motives (whether "mercy" or social "benefit") is a philosophy that the medical profession, as preservers of life, must never embrace and which a democratic and humanitarian society must never accept. It would involve climbing onto a greased slide from which no one can escape. If we can end the life of a hopeless cancer patient, then what is to stop us from acting similarly with the patient with hopeless brain damage or the senility of old age? What is to stop us from including the hopelessly mentally ill or retarded, or the bedridden who have become a burden to themselves and others? What of the incompetent patient who cannot give permission to terminate his life; who can decide his life is not worth living?

These superficially appealing euthanasia arguments have frightening corollaries and if they are accepted all our lives are in danger.

"The power of assisting the individual who elects to die with dignity should be vested in a board that is committed legally to respect the person's need and way of meeting it."

Individuals Should Have the Choice of Euthanasia

Margaret Mead

During her lifetime, Margaret Mead (1901-1978) was an anthropologist of worldwide renown. Her field studies in Bali and New Guinea resulted in the publication of numerous articles and books, many of which are considered classics. A graduate of Columbia University (PhD), for several years Dr. Mead held the prestigious position of curator of the American Museum of Natural History. In the following viewpoint, she explains why she believes that individuals should have the choice of euthanasia but only within a framework of commitment to the value of human life.

Consider the following questions while reading:
1. **What right should an incurably ill person have in the opinion of Dr. Mead?**
2. **What role should the doctor play in euthanasia decisions?**

Margaret Mead, "Margaret Mead Answers." Reprinted from **Redbook Magazine**, July, 1973. Copyright ©1973 by The McCall Publishing Company.

I do not believe that a society should have the power to decide that old people are useless or dispensible or no longer capable of living humanly and so end their lives. A society as such should not have this kind of power over human life, whether it is the old or the unborn, the feeble-minded or the desperately handicapped, whose lives are involved. It is our responsibility, especially in a society as rich as ours, to care for those who are in need of care.

It is true that among primitive peoples living on the edge of extinction—a small band of food gatherers in a period of extreme drought, for example—it may sometimes be necessary to decide who is to survive. But even in such cases we find that most societies try to save old people as long as they can or, as among the Eskimos, let them choose when it seems best to die.

EUTHANASIA PRESENTS SOME PROBLEMS

I do believe that a person who is very old or incurably ill should have that choice. But this also presents problems. At the point at which an old person no longer is able to relate in any way to his relatives and friends, he is not able to make the necessary decision. It now is advocated that the oxygen machine should be turned off when the brain is dead, even if the heart beats on; but someone must make the decision to turn off the machine.

Clearly the choice must be made long before the crisis occurs. And just as it is customary for people to make their last will and testament when they are well, in order to avoid the pressures and the forced or erratic decisions of a deathbed will, so also it is possible for persons to decide in advance and put in writing—as with a will—the circumstances under which they would want medical intervention and under what circumstances they would wish to have no further intervention.

I myself would wish to live as long as I could be a thinking and communicating person; I would not want to live as an uncommunicating body. As physicians generally respect the wishes of their patients who can make their decisions known, they also would be able to respect, with a clear conscience, the wishes their patients have set down earlier. And families would not be guiltridden about decisions made long before.

A further difficulty arises for the old person who does not need special medical intervention merely to keep him or her alive but who faces inevitable deterioration, pain and personal-

THE LIVING WILL

TO MY FAMILY, MY PHYSICIAN, MY LAWYER, MY CLERGYMAN

TO ANY MEDICAL FACILITY IN WHOSE CARE I HAPPEN TO BE

TO ANY INDIVIDUAL WHO MAY BECOME RESPONSIBLE FOR MY HEALTH, WELFARE OR AFFAIRS

Death is as much a reality as birth, growth, maturity and old age—it is the one certainty of life. If the time comes when I, _____ _____ can no longer take part in decisions for my own future, let this statement stand as an expression of my wishes, while I am still of sound mind.

If the situation should arise in which there is no reasonable expectation of my recovery from physical or mental disability, I request that I be allowed to die and not be kept alive by artificial means or "heroic measures". I do not fear death itself as much as the indignities of deterioration, dependence and hopeless pain. I, therefore, ask that medication be mercifully administered to me to alleviate suffering even though this may hasten the moment of death.

This request is made after careful consideration. I hope you who care for me will feel morally bound to follow its mandate. I recognize that this appears to place a heavy responsibility upon you, but it is with the intention of relieving you of such responsibility and of placing it upon myself in accordance with my strong convictions, that this statement is made.

Signed _____

Date _____

Witness _____

Witness _____

Copies of this request have been given to _____

_____

_____

_____

The Living Will, prepared by the Euthanasia Educational Council, directs the signer's family to avoid the use of extraordinary measures to maintain life in terminal illness.

ity distortion. There is at present a group advocating legislation to permit a physician to give a pill, at the request of the patient, that would give release from the suffering ahead. I believe it is the right of an individual to choose not to endure destructive suffering that can end only in death.

PHYSICIANS SHOULD NOT BEAR THE BURDEN

But I also believe we should not put on practicing physicians the double burden of being honest with their patients—and their patients' families—in telling them what lies ahead and of assisting their patients to end their lives. In a great many early cultures the power to cure and the power to kill were lodged in the same person. It was a great step forward in the history of medicine when care and curing were separated from any other power, and I do not think we should do anything to jeopardize this dedication of the physician to the life and well-being of his individual patients.

The power of assisting the individual who elects to die with dignity should be vested in a board that is committed legally to respect the person's need and way of meeting it. Such a board would have to be made up of persons with medical training—for example, public-health officials—but not men and women engaged in the medical care of the individual.

I believe individuals should have the choice of euthanasia. But such a choice must be set within a framework of ethical commitment to the value of human life.

"Instead of changing the law to make it legal to weed out us 'vegetables,' let us change the laws so that we may receive quality medical care, education, and freedom to live as full and productive lives as our potentials allow."

The Physically Disabled Have a Right To Life

Sondra Diamond

Sondra Diamond is a counseling psychologist who has had cerebral palsy since birth. The following viewpoint, originally entitled "On Being Alive," was introduced on the floor of the U.S. Senate by Senator Orrin Hatch of Utah (September 27, 1978). In it, Ms. Diamond explains the three ways euthanasia threatens the disabled and argues that the physically handicapped can and should be allowed to enjoy a full and happy life.

Consider the following questions while reading:
1. **Why does Ms. Diamond disagree with doctors who believe babies with birth defects should be allowed to die?**
2. **How does Ms. Diamond believe laws should be changed to affect the disabled?**
3. **In what three ways does Ms. Diamond assert the right to life issue affects the disabled?**

I have been physically disabled since birth as a result of brain damage. My disability is called Cerebral Palsy. Many people believe that Cerebral Palsy is synonymous with mental retardation. However, this is not true. When I was born my parents were told that I would never be able to speak, hear or do anything that other children could do. It was suggested that I be put away in an institution. My parents, however, felt that I had as much potential as their two older children.

"SHALL THIS CHILD DIE?"

In the November 12th, 1973 issue of *Newsweek* Magazine in the Medicine section, there appeared an article titled "Shall This Child Die?" It was about the work of Doctors Raymond S. Duff and A. G. M. Campbell at the Yale-New Haven Hospital of Yale University. The article reported that these doctors were permitting babies born with birth defects to die by deliberately withholding vital medical treatments. The doctors were convincing the parents of these children that they would be a final burden; that they had "Little or no hope of achieving meaningful 'humanhood'." The doctors recognized that they were breaking the law by doing away with these "vegetables," as they choose to call these children, but they felt that the law should be changed to make it legal to let these children die.

I was incensed by this article in *Newsweek*, although I was glad that the subject finally was coming above ground. For I had been aware of this practice for many years.

Feeling that I had to do something about this article, I wrote a Letter to the Editor of *Newsweek* Magazine. It was published in the December 3rd, 1973 issue, as follows:

"I'll wager my entire root system and as much fertilizer as it would take to fill Yale University that you have never received a letter from a vegetable before this one, but, much as I resent the term, I must confess that I fit the description of a "vegetable" as defined in the article 'Shall This Child Die?' (Medicine, Nov. 12).

"Due to severe brain damage incurred at birth, I am unable to dress myself, toilet myself, or write; my secretary is typing this letter. Many thousands of dollars had to be spent on my rehabilitation and education in order for me to reach my present professional status of a Counseling Psychologist. My parents were also told, 35 years ago, that there was 'little or no hope of achieving meaningful "humanhood"' for their daughter. Have I reached 'humanhood'? Compared with Doctors Duff and Campbell I believe I have surpassed it!

32

"Instead of changing the law to make it legal to weed out us 'vegetables,' let us change the laws so that we may receive quality medical care, education, and freedom to live as full and productive lives as our potentials allow."

SECOND CLASS CITIZENS

The physically disabled in our society have historically been second class citizens. And, as such, they have been subject to the same indignities that other minority groups have had to endure. Some 10 percent of the population of the United States is physically disabled. And that figure is merely an estimate, for these are the people who are on record in hospitals, agencies, and the like.

For most able-bodied people, willingness to contemplate the problems of the physically disabled is tempered by the fact that they have a set of notions and feelings about people different from themselves, whether they be of a different race, nationality, sex—or the physically disabled. I am, of course, especially interested in the feelings about the physically disabled. These feelings cannot be ignored; they must be faced head-on.

A TIME TO DIE

Who should make the decision for or against euthanasia if the patient himself is mentally or physically incompetent to do so? His doctor? A committee of doctors? A court or some other agency of government? The next of kin?...

Can anyone other than God really be sure that a human being has reached his time to die?

Louis Cassels, *United Press International.*

Being disabled is not the same as thinking about what it would be like if you were disabled. Being disabled is not intrinsically a burden. It only becomes so when society makes it difficult to function as a normal person. Technology allows the disabled to move about and function freely. It is only

33

when society says *stop* that a physical disability becomes a handicap. In view of the fact society sees a physical disability as a burden, it is, for many, a natural assumption that the physically disabled would be better off dead. I cannot agree with such a solution.

Perhaps we should take a closer look at how I feel about being disabled. What is it like to be disabled? It's happy, it's sad, it's exciting, it's frustrating, it's probably just like being non-disabled. You worry what will become of you when your parents are no longer around to help you with your special needs. You want to go places and do things just like everyone else. You have the same sexual drives, the same hopes and dreams for marriage and a family, the same aspirations of a successful life...

HOW EUTHANASIA AFFECTS DISABLED

The right to life issue affects the disabled in three principal ways: *first, there is negative euthanasia which is practiced on newborn infants who are born with physical disabilities and abnormalities.* When a child is born with a disability, many members of the medical profession do not administer the necessary supportive medical services. It is argued that the child will be physically disabled the rest of its life anyway. If this were to be done to a child who would not grow up to be disabled, the courts would intervene. There have been many cases where the parents, for reasons such as religion, have not wanted their new born infant to receive medical care. Court orders have been obtained by the physicians so that they could perform the necessary procedures.

Second, euthanasia affects the physically disabled when we are hospitalized for medical problems other than our disabilities. To give you a personal example: in 1962 I was severely burned over 60% of my body by 3rd degree burns. When I was taken to the hospital the doctors felt that there was no point in treating me because I was disabled anyway and could not lead a normal life. They wanted to let me die. My parents, after a great deal of arguing, convinced the doctors that I was a junior in college and had been leading a normal life. However, they had to bring in pictures of me swimming and playing the piano. The Doctors were not totally convinced that this was the best procedure — grafting skin and giving me medication as they would with other patients — but my parents insisted that I be ministered to. Mine was not an unusual case. To take the time and effort to expend medical expertise on a person who is physically dis-

abled seems futile to many members of the medical profession. Their handiwork will come to nought, they think.

The third way euthanasia affects the physically disabled is when a person in adulthood becomes disabled. There are two parts to this problem. Firstly, should that person be treated and rehabilitated if he is not going to lead a normal life? Secondly, what if that person asks to die? If you have never been disabled you are not aware of the many options in life. Therapeutic rehabilitation techniques, self-help devices, and prosthetic and assistive equipment make the lives of the disabled very functional. It takes a great deal of time to discover these things. First the medical problem must be overcome and this is up to the medical profession. It is only after the critical period of illness that a rehabilitation team can take over. If a person who knows that he will be disabled for the rest of his life asks to die, it sounds like an attractive option to his family: Why should he have to suffer? Intensive psychological counseling is needed to show the individual who will be physically disabled (and his family) that life holds a great deal of potential. We cannot deny that there will be problems, but one can enjoy a full and happy life even though physically disabled. I would not give up one moment of life in which I could have another cup of coffee, another cigarette, or another interaction with someone I love.

Many people ask me about the person who is so severely disabled that he or she can only lie in bed. Shouldn't he be allowed to die? they ask me. We cannot know what is going on in that person's head — especially if he cannot communicate with us through speech. Perhaps he is enjoying the sensual experience of lying on cool sheets or the pleasure of good food, or being held by another human being...

We have posed the problem of euthanasia and its effects on the physically disabled. What can be done to alleviate this problem?

ALLEVIATING THE PROBLEM

First of all, as I said, you must face your feelings about the physically disabled — the negative ones as well as the positive ones. For you are human beings and must not think "I shouldn't feel this way." In the abstract it is easier to fight against abortion, infanticide, and euthanasia if we know that these children will grow up to be whole human beings. Physical attractiveness has become very important in our society. What I am asking you to do is fight abortion, infanticide, and euthanasia on behalf of people who will be, or are, physically disabled. You cannot begin to do this until you throw away your prejudices and preconceived notions about the life of a physically disabled person.

I have concentrated here on the obvious ways euthanasia threatens the disabled, because those dangers are of course most obvious to me. I know that, for most people, the right to life issue means primarily saving the lives of the unborn from abortion. But there is a least common denominator: life itself. It is the right of the disabled to appreciate the gift of life, to celebrate it *for* itself. Thus I think we can help you. I know we *want* to help you, every bit as much as we want you to help us.

"It is harder morally to justify letting somebody die a slow and ugly death, dehumanized, than it is to justify helping him escape from such misery."

The Case for Euthanasia

Joseph Fletcher

Joseph Fletcher is an educator and clergyman who is currently on the faculty of the Graduate School of Biomedical Sciences, University of Texas. The author of numerous books including *Situation Ethics* (1966) and *Humanhood: Essays in Biomedical Ethics* (1978), he was formerly Dean of St. Paul's Cathedral, Cincinnati and Professor of Social Ethics, Episcopal Theology School, Cambridge, Massachusetts. In the following viewpoint, Dr. Fletcher questions whether compassion is sufficient moral justification for suicide or euthanasia and concludes by answering "yes."

Consider the following questions while reading:
1. Why does Dr. Fletcher feel that the horror of Nazi Germany's euthanasia practices do not apply to our country's discussion of euthanasia?
2. What does Dr. Fletcher mean when he says that "it is *personal* function that counts, not *biological* function?"
3. What four forms of euthanasia does the author describe?
4. What does the author feel is the highest good and how does it relate to euthanasia?

Joseph Fletcher, "Ethics and Euthanasia," *To Live and To Die: When, Why, and How,* ed. Robert H. Williams (New York: Springer-Verlag, 1973). Reprinted with permission from Springer-Verlag.

It is harder morally to justify letting somebody die a slow and ugly death, dehumanized, than it is to justify helping him to escape from such misery. This is the case at least in any code of ethics which is humanistic or personalistic, i.e., in any code of ethics which has a value system that puts humanness and personal integrity above biological life and function. It makes no difference whether such an ethics system is grounded in a theistic or a naturalistic philosophy. We may believe that God wills human happiness or that man's happiness is, as Protagoras thought, a self-validating standard of the good and the right. But what counts ethically is whether human needs come first — not whether the ultimate sanction is transcendental or secular.

A MORAL DEFENSE OF EUTHANASIA

What follows is a moral defense of euthanasia. Primarily I mean active or positive euthanasia, which helps the patient to die, not merely the passive or negative form of euthanasia which "lets the patient go" by simply withholding life-preserving treatments. The plain fact is that negative euthanasia is already a fait accompli in modern medicine. Every day in a hundred hospitals across the land decisions are made clinically that the line has been crossed from prolonging genuinely human life to only prolonging subhuman dying, and when that judgment is made respirators are turned off, life-perpetuating intravenous infusions stopped, proposed surgery canceled, and drugs countermanded. So-called "Code 90" stickers are put on many record-jackets, indicating "Give no intensive care or resuscitation." Arguing pro and con about negative euthanasia is therefore merely flogging a dead horse. Ethically, the issue whether we may "let the patient go" is as dead as Queen Anne.

Straight across the board of religious traditions there is substantial agreement that we are not morally obliged to preserve life in all terminal cases. (The religious-ethical defense of negative euthanasia is far more generally accepted by ministers and priests than medical people recognize or as yet even accept.) Humanist morality shows the same non-absolutistic attitude about preserving life. Indeed, not only Protestant, Catholic, and Jewish teaching take this stance, but it is also true of Buddhist, Hindu, and Moslem ethics. In short, the claim that we ought always to do everything we can to preserve any patient's life as long as possible is now discredited...

Given modern medicine's capabilities always to do what is

38

technically possible to prolong life would be morally inde-
fensible on any ground other than a vitalistic outlook; that is,
the opinion that biological survival is the first-order value and
that all other considerations, such as personality, dignity,
well-being, and self-possession, necessarily take second
place. Vestigial last-ditch pro-vitalists still mumble threaten-
ingly about "what the Nazis did," but in fact the Nazis never
engaged in euthanasia or mercy killing; what they did was
merciless killing, either genocidal or for ruthless experimental purposes.

THE ETHICAL AND THE PRE—ETHICAL

One way of putting this is to say that the traditional ethics
based on the sanctity of life — which was the classical
doctrine of medical idealism in its prescientific phases —
must give way to a code of ethics of the quality of life. This
comes about for humane reasons. It is a result of modern
medicine's successes, not failures. New occasions teach new
duties, time makes ancient good uncouth, as Whittier said...

If God's will (perhaps "specially revealed" in the Bible or
"generally revealed" in his Creation) is against any responsible human initiative in the dying process, or if sheer life is
believed to be, as such, more desirable than anything else,
then those who hold these axioms will not find much merit in
any case we might make for either kind of euthanasia —
positive or negative. If, on the other hand, the highest good is
personal integrity and human well-being, then euthanasia in
either form could or might be the right thing to do, depending
on the situation. This latter kind of ethics is the key to what
will be said in this chapter.

Let's say it again, clearly, for the sake of truly serious
ethical discourse. Many of us look upon living and dying as
we do upon health and medical care, as person-centered.
This is not a solely or basically biological understanding of
what it means to be "alive" and to be "dead." It asserts that a
so-called "vegetable," the brain-damaged victim of an auto
accident or a microcephalic newborn or a case of massive
neurologic deficit and lost cerebral capacity, who nevertheless goes on breathing and whose midbrain or brain stem
continues to support spontaneous organ functions, is in such
a situation no longer a human being, no longer a person, no
longer really alive. It is personal function that counts, not
biological functions. Humanness is understood as primarily
rational, not physiological. This "doctrine of man" puts the
homo and ratio before the vita. It holds that being human is

39

more "valuable" than being alive.

All of this is said just to make it clear from the outset that biomedical progress is forcing us, whether we welcome it or not, to make fundamental conceptual changes as well as scientific and medical changes. Not only are the conditions of life and death changing, because of our greater control and in consequence our greater decision-making responsibility, our definitions of life and death also have to change to keep pace with the new realities...

CRIMINAL LAW vs. PATIENT'S LIBERTY

The criminal law should not be invoked to repress conduct unless this is demonstrably necessary on social grounds. What social interest is there in preventing the sufferer from choosing to accelerate his death by a few months? What positive value does his life still possess for society, that he is to be retained in it by the terrors of the criminal law?

And, of course, the liberty involved is that of the doctor as well as that of the patient. It is the doctor's responsibility to do all he can to prolong worth-while life, or, in the last resort, to ease his patient's passage. If the doctor honestly and sincerely believes that the best service he can perform for his suffering patient is to accede to his request for euthanasia, it is a grave thing that the law should forbid him to do so.

Granville Williams, "'Mercy Killing' Legislation — A Rejoinder", *Minnesota Law Review*, 1958.

CHOOSING DEATH

Genetics, molecular biology, fetology, and obstetrics have developed to a point where we now have effective control over the start of human life's continuum. And therefore from now on it would be irresponsible to leave babymaking to mere

Joseph Fletcher

chance and impulse, as we once had to do. Modern men are trying to face up in a mature way to our emerging needs of quality control — medically, ecologically, legally, socially.

What has taken place in birth control is equally imperative in death control. The whole armory of resuscitation and pro- longation of life forces us to be responsible decision makers about death as much as about birth; there must be quality control in the terminating of life as in its initiating. It is ridicu- lous to give ethical approval to the positive ending of sub- human life in utero, as we do in therapeutic abortions for reasons of mercy and compassion, but refuse to approve of positively ending a subhuman life in extremis. If we are morally obliged to put an end to a pregnancy when an amniocentesis reveals a terribly defective fetus, we are equally obliged to put an end to a patient's hopeless misery when a brain scan reveals that a patient with cancer has advanced brain metastases...

Only man is aware of death. Animals know pain, and fear it, but not death. Furthermore, in humans the ability to meet death and even to regard it sometimes as a friend is a sign of manliness. But in the new patterns of medicine and health care patients tend to die in a moribund or comatose state, so that death comes without the patient's knowledge. The Elizabethan litany's petition, "...from sudden death, good Lord, deliver us," has become irrelevant much if not most of the time.

It is because of this "incompetent" condition of so many of the dying that we cannot discuss the ethical issues of elective death only in the narrow terms of voluntary, patient-chosen euthanasia. A careful typology of elective death will distinguish at least four forms — ways of dying which are not merely willy-nilly matters of blind chance but of choice, purpose, and responsible freedom...

1. Euthanasia, or a "good death," can be voluntary and direct, i.e., chosen and carried out by the patient. The most familiar way is the overdose left near at hand for the patient. It is a matter of simple request and of personal liberty. If it can be held in the abortion debate that compulsory pregnancy is unjust and that women should be free to control their own bodies when others' lives (fetuses) are at stake, do not the same moral claims apply to control of the lives and bodies of people too? In any particular case we might properly raise the question of the patient's competence, but to hold that euthanasia in this category is justifiable entails a rejection of the simplistic canard that all suicide victims are mentally disordered.

Voluntary euthanasia is, of course, a form of suicide. Presumably a related issue arises around the conventional notion of consent in medical ethics. The codes (American Medical Association, Helsinki, World Medical Association, Nuremberg) all contend that valid consent to any surgery or treatment requires a reasonable prospect of benefit to the patient. What, then, is benefit? Could death in some situations be a benefit? My own answer is in the affirmative.

2. Euthanasia can be voluntary but indirect. The choice might be made either in situ or long in advance of a terminal illness, e.g., by exacting a promise that if and when the "bare bodkin" or potion cannot be self-administered somebody will do it for the patient. In this case the patient gives to others — physicians, lawyers, family, friends — the discretion to end it all and when the situation requires, if the patient becomes comatose or too dysfunctioned to make the decision...

3. Euthanasia may be direct but involuntary. This is the form in which a simple "mercy killing" is done on a patient's behalf without his present or past request. Instances would be when an idiot is given a fatal dose or the death of a child in the worst stages of Tay-Sachs disease is speeded up, or when a man trapped inextricably in a blazing fire is shot to end his suffering, or a shutdown is ordered on a patient deep in mindless condition, irreversibly, perhaps due to an injury or an infection or some biological breakdown...

4. Finally, euthanasia might be both indirect and involuntary. This is the "letting the patient go" tactic which is taking place every day in our hospitals. Nothing is done for the patient positively to release him from his tragic condition (other than "trying to make him comfortable"), and what is done negatively is decided for him rather than in response to his request...

But ethically regarded, this indirect-involuntary form of euthanasia is manifestly superficial, morally timid, and evasive of the real issue. I repeat: it is harder morally to justify letting somebody die a slow and ugly death, dehumanized, than it is to justify helping him to avoid it.

MEANS AND ENDS

What, then, is the real issue? In a few words, it is whether we can morally justify taking it into our own hands to hasten death for ourselves (suicide) or for others (mercy killing) out of reasons of compassion. The answer to this in my view is clearly Yes, on both sides of it. Indeed, to justify either one, suicide or mercy killing, is to justify the other.

The heart of the matter analytically is the question of whether the end justifies the means. If the end sought is the patient's death as a release from pointless misery and dehumanization, then the requisite or appropriate means is justified. Immanuel Kant said that if we will the end we will the means. The old maxim of some moral theologians was finis sanctificat media. The point is that no act is anything but random and meaningless unless it is purposefully related to

43

some end or object. To be moral an act must be seeking an end...

The really searching question of conscience is, therefore, whether we are right in believing that the well-being of persons is the highest good. If so, then it follows that either suicide or mercy killing could be the right thing to do in some exigent and tragic circumstances. This could be the case, for instance, when an incorrigible "human vegetable," whether spontaneously functioning or artificially supported, is progressively degraded while constantly eating up private or public financial resources in violation of the distributive justice owed to others. In such cases the patient is actually already departed and only his body is left, and the needs of others have a stronger claim upon us morally...

Another way of putting this is to say that the crucial question is not whether the end justifies the means (what else could?) but what justifies the end? And this chapter's answer is, plainly and confidently, that human happiness and well-being is the highest good or summum bonum, and that therefore any ends or purposes which that standard or ideal validates are just, right, good. This is what humanistic medicine is all about; it is what the concepts of loving concern and social justice are built upon...

A WELCOME OPTION OF DEATH

There is one issue, however, on which a broad consensus appears to have been achieved: the final moments of a life should not be degrading to the one who has lived it. The possibility of dying with dignity should come as a welcome option to us all.

William E. Steel, *The Christian Century*, November 17, 1976.

The plain hard logic of it is that the end or purpose of both negative and positive euthanasia is exactly the same: to contrive or bring about the patient's death. Acts of deliberate omission are morally not different from acts of commission. But in the Anglo-American law, it is a crime to push a blind man off the cliff. It is not, however, a crime to deliberately not lift a finger to prevent his walking over the edge...

Careful study of the best texts of the Hippocratic Oath shows that it says nothing at all about preserving life, as such. It says that "so far as power and discernment shall be mine, I will carry out regimen for the benefit of the sick and will keep them from harm and wrong." The case for euthanasia depends upon how we understand "benefit of the sick" and "harm" and "wrong." If we regard dehumanized and merely biological life as sometimes real harm and the opposite of benefit, to refuse to welcome or even introduce death would be quite wrong morally.

In most states in this country people can and do carry cards, legally established (by Anatomical Gift Acts), which explain the carrier's wish that when he dies his organs and tissue should be used for transplant when needed by the living. The day will come when people will also be able to carry a card, notarized and legally executed, which explains that they do not want to be kept alive beyond the humanum point, and authorizing the ending of their biological processes by any of the methods of euthanasia which seems appropriate.

"The starting point of medical ethics is proper respect for the human person. This implies the moral obligation to preserve health and prolong life."

The Case Against Euthanasia

Leonard J. Weber

Leonard J. Weber is currently an associate professor of philosophy and religion at Mercy College, Detroit. He received his MA in theology from Marquette University and his PhD in Religious Studies from McMaster University, Hamilton, Ontario. A member of the American Academy of Religion and the American Society for Christian Ethics, Dr. Weber has authored two books including *Who Shall Live? The Dilemma of Severely Handicapped Children and Its Meaning for Other Moral Questions* (1972). In the following viewpoint, he criticizes Joseph Fletcher's defense of euthanasia and argues that there is always evil in the act of killing.

Consider the following questions while reading:

1. How does the author answer the question "What is a human person?" How is his answer important to the debate on euthanasia?
2. What position does the author take on the "sanctity of life" versus the "quality of life" controversy?

Leonard Weber, "Ethics and Euthanasia: Another View," *American Journal of Nursing,* July, 1973. Copyright July, 1973, The American Journal of Nursing Company. Reprinted from *American Journal of Nursing.* Condensed with permission of the American Journal of Nursing Company.

In his moral defense of euthanasia, Joseph Fletcher challenged many basic elements of the traditional ethical view of mercy killing. Such a challenge should not be unanswered; the matter is too important...

PERSONALISTIC ETHICS

Dr. Fletcher argues that for anyone who accepts a personalistic and humanistic code of ethics, it is harder to justify letting someone die slowly than it is to give him a lethal injection. At the heart of his defense for directly killing certain patients who are terminally ill is his concept of a personalistic approach to ethics. This concept must be examined and seriously questioned.

Without a doubt, the human person must be the concern of ethics and medicine. The only proper care of a patient is to treat him as a person, a whole person, and not just as a specimen of biological life. A fundamental principle of medical ethics is that people be treated with respect; violation of the human person, thus, is unethical.

But what is a human person? A person is made up of components that are personal and physical, spiritual and corporeal. In traditional language a person is body and soul. The two cannot be separated in man as we know him. Man is an embodied being, the body of his spirit no less than the spirit of his body. The spirit may survive the death of the body, but the only person medicine ever knows is an embodied being. The human person, then,. is violated when either the body or the personality is violated.

Ethicists like Dr. Fletcher appear to so emphasize the personality side of man that they tend to lose respect for the physical and to deny that a violation of the physical is a violation of the human person...

It is this neglect of the value of the physical dimension of man that is behind Dr. Fletcher's defense of direct euthanasia. He is right to advocate a personalistic ethic, but his notion of what constitutes a human person is too one-sided. A more adequate personalistic ethic would see the physical as worthy of respect...It would be most strange if the medical profession accepted a system of ethics that denies value to the body.

Ethicists who understand the person to be a combination of the spiritual and the physical are not particularly uneasy with the practice of allowing a terminally ill patient to die (not considering the question of who does the deciding), but they will have a great deal of uneasiness with directly taking the life of a patient to end his misery. In other words, the moral distinction between killing and allowing to die can be defended as valid and essential.

MEDICAL ETHICS

The starting point of medical ethics is proper respect for the human person. This implies the moral obligation to preserve health and prolong life. These obligations are not without limits, however. Just as a person should not be considered pure personality, so should he not be considered simply body. It is the good of the total man that must be served.

There is little doubt that terminally ill patients often are best served by giving up attempts to extend their lives and, instead, concentrating on their needs as dying persons. We miss the point, I think, when we see ending the prolongation of life simply in terms of death. Respect for a dying person may demand that we stop the art of healing so that we can help the patient practice what medieval man called ars moriendi, the art of dying. The positive meaning of "allowing the patient to die" is the attempt to provide for a peaceful death in the midst of family, rather than having a patient die alone, because the family may interfere with the staff's fight to keep death at bay. Actually, a good case can be made for initiating this type of care for patients earlier than is usually done.

RIGHT TO BE PUT TO DEATH

It is often said that everyone has a right to a death with dignity... What it really means is a right to be put to death, and put to death by others, which in fact proposes the duty of others to kill. There are comparable difficulties with the argument that legalized euthanasia would mean an improvement in the quality of life. Clearly, the improvement is not experienced by those who are put to death...

Sonya Rudikoff, *Commentary*, February, 1974.

Giving up the fight against death does not show lack of respect for the physical dimension of human personhood. It merely says that the overall good of the patient can best be served, not by violating the physical, but by allowing an illness or injury to take its course. The same cannot be said about directly intervening in order to bring about a good death. Mercy killing is not discontinuation of the fight to extend life in order to serve the needs of the dying patient. Rather, mercy killing is the direct ending of the life of the patient. As such, it is a violation of the person. It is a human agent, not a disease that is the immediate cause of death. This type of difference should not be ignored.

SANCTITY OF LIFE

Dr. Fletcher advocates an ethics based upon an emphasis on the quality of life in opposition to the traditional ethics based upon the conviction of the sanctity of life. It is true that there may be some difficulty with the sanctity-of-life concept, a difficulty that arises especially when we consider self-defense. Yet the basic elements of the sanctity-of-life ethics are essential for ethical living and cannot be set aside without weakening man's respect for man. Each person's life is sacred, beyond the realm of legitimate interference by another; all lives are of equal value. These are the primary premises of a sanctity-of-life ethics. There is no need to prove one's right to life and there is no justification for saying that the taking of one person's life is less of an evil than the taking of another's. Some such starting point would seem to be necessary if we are to respect a person because of the very fact that he is a person.

A quality-of-life ethics implies that only some lives are valuable and that only some lives are worthy of the respect that condemns physical violation. A quality-of-life ethics has an admirable goal: it sets out to improve the manner of human living. Yet it gets into trouble as soon as it opposes the quality of life against the sanctity of life. It immediately denies that the fact of human life is sufficient reason for inviolability; it ends by saying that some lives can be taken...

The sanctity-of-life approach is also concerned about the quality of human life. The quality of all our lives suffers, it insists, unless every human life is considered inviolable because of the very fact of its existence. A dying patient's relationship to those about him symbolizes the relationship of all men to one another. To practice direct euthanasia, even at the request of the patient, is to weaken the claim of each one of us to the right to have others respect and not violate us. Man is more than just spirit, and there are more ways of

49

being violated than having one's free will coerced.

There is an enormous difference between not fighting death and actively putting an end to life. The former is fully compatible with respect for human life. The latter, while done with the best of intentions, is logically part of the view that human life itself is not enough to warrant our respect. The former is fully compatible with the humanistic nature of medicine itself. The latter could seem to be introducing a dehumanizing element into the medical profession.

ENDS AND MEANS

At the heart of the ethics of euthanasia lies the question of whether the end justifies the means. For Dr. Fletcher, the end (that is, purpose) most assuredly does justify the means. For this reason, euthanasia is considered good and for this reason there is no ethical difference between directly killing a patient and allowing him to die. In both cases, he contends, the end sought is the patient's release from pointless misery. This end is good and, therefore, the action necessary to bring about this end is also good...

The primary difficulty with this position is that the emphasis is on the purpose, the intention, the why of acting, and not enough on the nature of the action...

EUTHANASIA AND SUFFERING

The scope that legalized euthanasia would give for fraud and foul play must also be realistically assessed, and the question asked: Whose suffering is to be alleviated, that of the patient or that of the relatives? Self-deception is a constant danger, and an apparently humanitarian motive may be only a cloak for selfishness.

Norman St. John-Stevas, *America*, May 31, 1975.

But acts have a moral quality, regardless of intention or purpose. Actions are not meaningless morally until purposely related to an end by man. By their very nature, actions produce consequences that often enhance or attack the well-being; the very action is evil. Now, intentions and circumstances are important. Killing in war, cold-blooded murder, and mercy killing are all different, morally speaking, because the circumstances are different. Yet there always is evil in the act of killing — the evil of rendering a previously alive person dead — and this evil is the starting point for all considerations of the morality of any kind of killing...

The principle that the proposed end justifies the means is found in a system of ethics that makes the mind of man the basis of morality. And to say that the mind of man is the basis of morality is to put man at the center of the meaning of the universe, a place which he does not truly occupy.

It sometimes seems as though there is a giant contradiction in the thinking of the modern Western world. In our understanding of the physical universe, we have experienced the Copernican revolution. In our understanding of the moral universe we are tending to do just the opposite: we are going from a world view that sees man as living morally by finding the meaning of the universe and conforming himself to it to the view that man himself, in his intentions, is the source and center of moral meaning. Fortunately, the moral reversal of the Copernican revolution is not accepted by all.

One does not have to believe in God in order to recognize that the meaning of the universe does not come from man's mind (though such a belief often helps). The recent ecological emphasis is, in part, an awareness of the fact that man is simply not being true to the facts when he acts as though he can give whatever meaning he wants to the world about him.

MEDICINE THROUGH SCIENCE AND TECHNOLOGY

Modern medicine, with its tremendously increased ability to preserve life and restore health, has demonstrated the good that can be accomplished through science and technology. It must be careful, though, that it does not accept an attitude that often accompanies scientific and technological work: that nature has no meaning in itself and that such things as living and dying become meaningful in terms of human purpose and human control. The inadequacies and dangers of such an attitude are apparent.

When viewed in the context we have just been examining, direct euthanasia seems to be more closely related to

Leonard J. Weber

prolonging life by all possible means than to allowing the patient to die.

Prolonging life as long as possible and directly bringing about death by mercy killing are both examples of attempts to control the living and dying processes to the greatest extent possible. Ceasing attempts to prolong life medically can, on the other hand, follow from quite a different attitude. What is being done in this case can be very much in tune with the idea that, at times, the most human way to act is to refuse to attempt to control life and death any further.

Just as human life does not have to prove its value by anyone's requirements for human personhood, so death does not have to be given meaning by the administration of a lethal injection at just the proper time. The decision not to resuscitate is fully compatible with respect for the fullness of human meaning. The administration of a lethal overdose is not.

ABILITY TO EMPATHIZE

The ability to empathize, to see life and its problems through another person's eyes, is a skill you must develop if you intend to learn from the experience of others.

Consider the following true life situation:

THE PREMATURE MONGOLOID*

Seven months along in her pregnancy, Mrs. Phyllis Obernauer woke up one morning feeling warm. She couldn't believe it, but she felt she was ready to deliver. As the Obernauers reached the hospital parking lot, Paul heard a gushing sound in the back seat. He turned around to see his baby daughter on the floor of the car.

For the next 24 hours, the hospital staff seemed to avoid her, Phyllis recalls, and even her obstetrician failed to visit her. She sensed something was wrong, but no one would say what. Finally, the crushing news: her premature daughter was not only mongoloid but had a hole in her heart and major intestinal blockage. The child gasped for every breath because of the heart problem and vomited everything it was fed because of the blockage. An operation would have to be performed immediately to correct the blockage or the baby would die.

Paul Wilkes, *Life Magazine*, Copyright ©1972 Time Inc. Reprinted with permission of the publisher. *Mongolism is more properly referred to as Downs Syndrome.

"To me, this wasn't a birth, it was an ejection," Mrs. Obernauer, mother of three other, healthy girls, says in a weary voice. "It was an imperfect fetus that my body wanted to get rid of. I looked ahead to the life this child would lead as a mongoloid, the expense of the hospitalization and the heart surgery someday. I looked at the terrific strain it would place on our girls and even more on our already shaky marriage, and I made a decision I didn't think I was capable of, I told them to let the baby die."

Phyllis recalls that the hospital staff was horrified by her attitude. "They hated me. But I would be the one saddled with this...this thing."

Her wish to allow the baby to die was not carried out. The local bureau of children's services obtained a court order and forced the intestinal operation. After $4,000 in bills, two months of intensive care — including intravenous feedings and massive doses of antibiotics to remedy a staph infection that blew up the baby's stomach like a balloon — the child was declared fit to go home.

"At first I wasn't going to pick her up from the hospital," Phyllis recalls. "But the word got around, and my 11-year-old daughter Audrey told me one of her friends had said, 'What a mommy you have. Won't even bring home her own baby.'" When the parents finally brought the child home, the Medicaid card issued read starkly, "OBERNAUER, BABY G." The Obernauers have steadfastly refused to name the baby, but call her Tara, after a character Phyllis saw on a soap opera.

Neighbors did their best to cheer Phyllis up. Some baked cookies, others brought toys for the baby, many spent hours sitting and talking. "One day I was introduced to this Presbyterian minister and I wondered why," she says. "Spiritual help? No, he had two mongoloid children and somehow I was supposed to see how blessed I was with one. But the children took to Tara and that's the toughest part. Just last night she had a hard time breathing and I found her in bed with Audrey this morning, with Holly — she's 9 — and Bonnie, 6, cooing over her.

"My husband's father was in a German concentration camp, so we Jews know to what extent 'mercy killings' can go. But why, when there are too many people in the world, keep alive an unwanted, malformed child? I've read all the books about mongoloid children, and the mothers tell of the love and affection and all. But it's like having a pet, not a human being. Many of the books conclude that death would be better."

Because of Phyllis's attitude, a social worker visited her new, sparsely furnished home in Chester, N.J. once a month for about half a year to make sure she didn't mistreat the baby. "What can my children think of their mother when this state car pulls up to check on her?" she says. "The bureaucracy, the state make me sick. I told them they saved the baby, they could keep her. But if they institutionalize the baby, we'd have to pay $200 a month. My husband just lost his drugstore business and we're just barely making it now." Paul Obernauer, who works as a pharmacist, and his wife have had stormy months since the child was born. In the anguish and confusion, each has blamed the other for the child and they have seriously considered divorce...

A doctor recently recommended that the baby might be helped by an experimental muscle-strengthening drug, but Phyllis refuses to consider it. "I'll do no more for the child than clean and feed and dress her."

"We don't think what it will be like a year or even a month from now. In one sense I'm sitting at home waiting for this child to die. If she gets pneumonia I don't think I'd rush her to the hospital. But that's tougher to say as each day goes by. The decision to let a child like this die must be made — and respected — before there is any attachment. But I still say, if there was a place where I could take this child today, and she would be put to sleep permanently, I would do it."

INSTRUCTIONS

Try to imagine how the following individuals would react to this situation.
What reasons do you think they would give for their actions?
Try to imagine and explain their feelings.

Mrs. Obernauer

Mr. Obernauer

Tara's sisters

Tara at the age of 16 (if she lives)

Mrs. Obernauer's doctor

The hospital staff

Joseph Fletcher (Author of Viewpoint 5, Chapter 1)

Leonard Weber (Author of Viewpoint 6, Chapter 1)

YOU

BIBLIOGRAPHY

The following list of periodical articles deals with the subject matter of this chapter.

T. Daniels

Nurse's Tale: Mercy Killing Decisions, **New York,** April 30, 1979, p. 37.

M. Stanton Evans

Alarming Implications of the Quinlan Case, **Human Events,** July 17, 1976, p. 563.

R.A. McCormick and A.E. Hellegers

Legislation and the Living Will, **America,** March 12, 1977, p. 210.

J.W. Montgomery

Do We Have the Right to Die?," **Christianity Today,** January 26, 1977, p. 49.

J. Robert Nelson

The Question of Euthanasia, **Engage/Social Action Forum - 16,** April, 1976.

J.J. Paris

Brother Fox, The Courts and Death With Dignity, **America,** November 8, 1980, p. 282.

J.J. Paris

Death Dilemmas, **The Christian Century,** March 11, 1981, p. 253.

J.R.W. Scott

What Is Human Life Anyway?, **Christianity Today,** April 6, 1979, p. 32.

M.R. Skrocki

Final Choices, **McCalls,** July, 1979, p.54.

William E. Steel

The Right to Die: New Options in California, **The Christian Century,** November 17, 1976, p. 996.

Douglas K. Stuart

Mercy Killing — Is It Biblical?, **Christianity Today,** February 27, 1976, p. 9.

K. Vaux

Intending Death: Moral Perspectives, **The Christian Century,** January 26, 1977, p. 56.

Edward Wakin

Is the Right-to-Die Wrong?, **U.S. Catholic,** March, 1978, p.6.

Chapter 2

PROBLEMS OF DEATH

Should Abortions Be Permitted?

"The decision concerning abortion can be made only by an individual in accordance with her conscience, consistent with sound medical practices."

Why We Support Legalized Abortion

Religious Coalition for Abortion Rights

The Religious Coalition for Abortion Rights is comprised of 27 major Protestant, Jewish, Catholic and other religious organizations committed to safeguarding the option of legal abortion as guaranteed by the Supreme Court in January 1973. Although the member organizations hold widely varying views on when abortion is a moral alternative, all are agreed that individuals must have the right to make decisions concerning abortion based on their own conscience and religious beliefs, and in accordance with responsible medical practice.

Consider the following questions while reading:
1. **How did the 1973 Supreme Court decision affect abortions in the United States?**
2. **Why do these religious organizations favor legalized abortions?**

From an undated pamphlet by the Religious Coalition for Abortion Rights titled *Abortion: Why Religious Organizations In the United States Want to Keep It Legal.*

HISTORY OF AMERICAN ABORTION LAWS

Before the 1800's...the United States followed the traditional English practice of permitting abortions before "quickening" (when movement of the fetus is detected).

During the 1800's...legislatures in the states passed laws prohibiting abortion except to save the life of the mother. These laws were enacted to protect women from the dangerous surgical methods of the times, not to protect the fetus. Women resorted to illegal abortions, often risking their lives and health.

In the 1950's...the abortion reform movement began in the states and by 1970, 13 states permitted abortion under certain circumstances — such as in cases of rape, incest, fetal deformity, and for the protection of women's health. Four states adopted laws which removed practically all restrictions on abortions.

LOGO OF RELIGIOUS COALITION FOR ABORTION RIGHTS

In 1973...the United States Supreme Court overturned all of the state laws. It ruled that the decision concerning abortion in the first three months of pregnancy should be between a woman and her physician; in the second three months, only laws to protect maternal health could be passed by the states, and in the last three months, when the fetus is viable, the states could pass laws forbidding abortion, except where it is necessary to preserve the mother's life or health.

Since 1973...there has been a well-organized effort by a small but vocal minority to overturn the Supreme Court decision. For moral and religious reasons this group is against permitting abortion as one of the alternative solutions for problem pregnancies. It is working unceasingly for the passage of laws in the states and in the United States Congress which will prohibit entirely or severely limit the availability of legal abortions...

RELIGIOUS VIEWS OF THE ABORTION ISSUE

Differing Views. Religious faiths in the United States hold widely differing views on abortion. A few do not approve of abortion for any reason; some hold that abortion is justified only under certain circumstances; and still others believe that the decision should be made by the woman and her doctor.

Positions Reached Against Restrictive Laws. Over the past decade, most Protestant and Jewish organizations have reached positions which oppose restrictive *abortion laws*, because:

...restrictive laws are not just or enforceable,
...they compel many women either to have unwanted children or to seek illegal and often medically dangerous abortions; and
...they discriminate particularly against poor women.

Though they may hold differing views on the *morality of abortion*, these groups have concluded that the decision concerning abortion can be made only by an individual in accordance with her conscience, consistent with sound medical practices. They believe there should be no abortion laws which reflect any one particular religious viewpoint. Rather, the state should remain neutral, leaving each faith free to practice and teach its beliefs as guaranteed by the United States Constitution.

'You've been found guilty of being poor, female and raped, and we sentence you to nine months' hard labor'

Reprinted by permission of Mike Peters, *Dayton Daily News.*

Many Protestant and Jewish organizations worked to end the restrictive state abortion laws. Clergy of many faiths helped women to obtain safe and reasonably-priced abortions where prohibited. Known as the Clergy Consultation Service, these clergy, risking the penalty for violating criminal laws, counselled women in order to help them reach their own decisions and to minimize the fear and degradation which accompanied most illegal abortions.

RELIGIOUS SUPPORT OF ABORTION RIGHTS TODAY

Most of the Protestant and Jewish organizations in the United States believed that the 1973 Supreme Court ruling was the appropriate solution to the abortion issue because it removed the state from the abortion decision except for medical reasons. The present attempts by an organized minority to overturn the Court's ruling are seen by these groups as a threat to the constitutional rights of women and to freedom of religion.

"Abortions are always grisly tragedies."

Our Abortion Culture

Nick Thimmesch

Nick Thimmesch is a Washington based syndicated column-
ist for the New York newspaper, *Newsday*. A staunch
opponent of abortion, in the following viewpoint he maintains
that abortion impinges upon human dignity and warns that
the worst barbarisms have small beginnings.

Consider the following questions while reading:
1. **How does the author relate German medicine of the
   1930's to the abortion issue in our country today?**
2. **What dangers does Mr. Thimmesch see in some of the
   medical practices advocated in our country?**
3. **What is meant by the term "the utilitarian ethic"? Why
   does the author feel that it is not as much a threat in the
   United States as it was in Nazi Germany?**

Occasionally we come on to something that strikes the core and won't go away. For me, it has been the question of the value of human life — a question embracing abortion, letting the newborn die, euthanasia and the creeping utilitarian ethic in medicine that impinges on human dignity. It's all reminiscent of the "what is useful is good" philosophy of German medicine in the '30's — a utilitarianism that sent 275,000 "unworthy" Germans to death and helped bring on the Hitler slaughter of millions of human beings a few years later.

Now super-abortionists and others who relish monkeying around with human life cry that this is scare stuff inspired by hysterical Catholics waving picket signs. Not so. There is growing concern among Protestant and Jewish thinkers about "right to life" and the abortion-binge mentality.

Fetal life has become cheap... The abortion culture is upon us. In one operating room, surgeons labor to save a 21-week-old baby; in the next, surgeons destroy, by abortion, another child, who can also be reckoned to be 21 weeks old. Where is the healing?

PLASTIC BAGS

Look beyond the political arguments and see the fetus and what doctors do to it. An unborn baby's heartbeat begins between the 18th and 25th day; brain waves can be detected at seven weeks; at nine to ten weeks, the unborn squint, swallow and make a fist. Look at the marvelous photographs and see human life. Should these little human beings be killed unless it is to save the mother's life?

Other photos show this human life aborted, dropped onto surgical gauze or into plastic-bagged garbage pails. Take that human life by suction abortion and the body is torn apart, becoming a jumble of tiny arms and legs. In a D and C abortion, an instrument slices the body to pieces. Salt poisoning at nineteen weeks? The saline solution burns away the outer layer of the baby's skin. The ultimate is the hysterotomy (Caesarean section) abortion. As an operation, it can save mother and child; as an abortion it kills the child. Often, this baby fights for its life, breathes, moves and even cries. To see this, or the pictures of a plastic-bagged garbage can full of dead babies, well, it makes believers in right-to-life.

It's unfair to write this way, cry the super-abortionists, or to show the horrible photos. But Buchenwald and Dachau

64

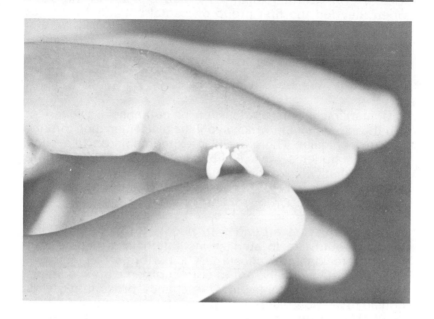

"Tiny Feet" *— Tiny human feet at ten weeks, perfectly formed.*

With permission, *Handbook On Abortion*, Wilke, Hiltz and Hayes Publishing Co., Inc.

looked terrible, too. Abortions are always grisly tragedies. This truth must be restated at a time when medical administrators chatter about "cost-benefit analysis" factors in deciding who lives and who dies.

THE 'GOOD DEATH'

The utilitarian ethic is also common in the arguments of euthanasia advocates at work in six state legislatures. Their euphemisms drip like honey (should I say, cyanide?) just as they did in Germany — "death with dignity," the "good death." Their legal arguments fog the mind. Their mentality shakes me. One doctor, discussing the suicide-prone, wrote: "In such instances, positive euthanasia — a nice, smooth anesthetic to terminate life — appears preferable to suicide." Dr. Russell Sackett, author of the "Death With Dignity" bill in Florida, said: "Florida has 1,500 mentally retarded and mentally ill patients, 90 per cent of whom should be allowed to die." The German utilitarians had concluded the same when they led the first group of mental patients to the gas chamber at the Sonnestein Psychiatric Hospital in 1939. It bothers me that eugenicists in Germany organized the mass destruction of mental patients, and in the United States pro-abortionists now also serve in pro-euthanasia organizations. Sorry, but I see a pattern.

Utilitarianism isn't all abortion or euthanasia. Utilitarians ran the experiment in which syphilitic black men died through lack of penicillin. There are also experiments on free-clinic patients, students, the institutionalized. Senate hearings revealed that two experimental birth-control drugs were used on the "vulnerable" for purposes other than those approved by the Food and Drug Administration.

This monkeying around with people is relentless. Some medics would like to sterilize institutionalized people from here to breakfast. Psychosurgery is performed on hundreds of Americans annually, not to correct organic brain damage, but to alter their behavior. This chancy procedure, a first cousin of the now discredited prefrontal lobotomy that turned 50,000 Americans into human vegetables, is performed on unruly children and violence-prone prisoners.

FETAL EXPERIMENTATION

Experimenters produce life outside the womb — combining sperm and ovum — and dispose of the human zygotes by pouring the solution down the sink drain. Recently scientists debated guidelines for experimenting with the live human fetus. To those considering the fetus as an organ, like, say, a kidney, Dr. Andre Hellegers of Georgetown University pointed out that fetuses have their own organs and cannot be considered organs themselves. How does one get consent from a live fetus? he asked. Or even from its donors — the parents who authorized the abortion?

Once fetal experimentation is sanctioned, are children to be next? Farfetched? No. In the New England Journal of Medicine, Dr. Franz Ingelfinger recently advocated removing the World Medical Association's absolute ban on experimenting with children and mental incompetents.

We can brake the tendencies of technocratic-minded doctors and administrators coldly concerned with "cost-benefit analysis." There was no such brake in Germany. After the first killings at Sonnestein, respected German doctors, not Nazi officials, killed 275,000 patients in the name

Nick Thimmesch

of euthanasia. Many were curable. Eventually the doomed "undesirables" included epileptics, mental defectives, World War I amputees, children with "badly modeled ears" and "bed wetters."

UTILITARIAN ETHIC

The worst barbarisms often have small beginnings. The logical extension of this utilitarian ethic was the mass exterminations in slave-labor camps. In "A Sign for Cain," Dr. Frederic Wertham tells how death-dealing technicians from

German state hospitals (and their equipment) were moved to the camps in 1942 to begin the big job.

Could the "what is useful is good" mentality lead to such horror in the U.S.? Not so long as I am allowed to write like this — which German journalists couldn't. Not so long as right-to-life Americans can dispute — which Germans couldn't. The extremes of the utilitarian mentality rampaging today through medicine, the drug industry and government will be checked by our press, lawmakers and doctors, lawyers and clergymen holding to the traditional ethic. The Germans weren't blessed that way.

"In countries where abortion has been legal for years, there is no evidence that respect for life has diminished... Infanticide, however, is prevalent in countries where the overburdened poor cannot control their childbearing."

20 Myths About Abortion

National Abortion Rights Action League

The National Abortion Rights Action League (NARAL) is a pro-choice organization with affiliates throughout the United States. The following viewpoint is an excerpt from a position paper circulated by NARAL and prepared by Polly Rothstein of the Westchester Coalition for Legal Abortion. In it, a series of pro and con arguments on legalizing abortion are presented. The statements in bold print represent pro-life arguments. The statements following the bold print represent pro-choice rebuttals.

Consider the following questions while reading:

1. **How does this viewpoint answer the charge that "abortion should not be permitted because it is wrong?"**
2. **How does the viewpoint respond to the charge that "there are alternatives to abortion. Abortion is never necessary?"**

From an undated pamphlet by the National Abortion Rights Action League titled *Legal Abortion: Arguments Pro & Con.*

Human life begins at conception; therefore, abortion is murder of a person.

The belief in personhood at conception is a religious belief held by the Roman Catholic Church. Most Protestant and Jewish denominations regard the fetus as a POTENTIAL human being, not a full-fledged person, and have position statements in support of legal abortion. There is no consensus in the religious, legal, political or scientific communities as to when the unborn becomes a person. It is a matter of religion and values, not absolute fact.

Abortion should not be legal because it is wrong.

Most Americans believe that under some circumstances abortion may be the "right" choice for a woman, and motherhood may be the "wrong" choice. A woman should decide this for herself without government interference.

Use of term "pro-abortion" to refer to those who support legal abortion rights.

We do not recommend abortion; we support the right to choose legal abortion. We are for reproductive freedom; no one should be forced to have an abortion, and no one should be forced to have a baby...

Use of term "pro-life" to refer to those who oppose legal abortion.

The tactics and literature of those who oppose legal abortion make it clear that most are concerned only with fetal life. They are openly callous about women, unwanted babies, and the quality of life. Ironically, most anti-abortion members of Congress vote against medical and social welfare programs...

The Supreme Court ruled that abortion on demand is legal for the entire nine months of a pregnancy.

The Court did not give women "abortion on demand;" it must be a decision between a woman and her doctor. The states may prohibit abortion in the third trimester except to preserve the life or health of the woman. In actual practice, abortions are rarely, if ever, performed after viability of the fetus.

The "abortion mentality" leads to infanticide, euthanasia, and killing of retarded and elderly persons.

In countries where abortion has been legal for years, there is no evidence that respect for life has diminished or that legal abortion leads to killing of any persons. Infanticide, however, is prevalent in countries where the overburdened poor cannot control their childbearing, and was prevalent in Japan before

"IT'S PART OF THE PLAN TO FREE PEOPLE FROM GOVERNMENT INTERFERENCE"

abortion was legalized.

Abortion is being used as a solution to population problems.
Women choose abortion for personal reasons. Reproduc-

tive freedom may help lower a country's birth rate, but in the most humane way possible...

Our government can't afford to give poor women free abortions on demand. The poor aren't entitled to everything the rich have, anyhow.

Cutting off Medicaid for abortion would cost the taxpayers much more in the long run for the birth and years of welfare for the woman and child. It is a distortion to treat abortion as a luxury item. Since our government has already decided to provide necessary medical care for the poor, it should not retreat selectively from this humane public policy...

Legalized abortion is a sign of the moral decay of a country.

That is an argument of the right wing fringe, who believe that their morality is the best or only one, and should be written into the law. Most people believe that it is immoral to force women to choose between unwanted babies and illegal abortions...

Women have abortions for their own convenience or on "whim."

Right-to-Life dismisses unwanted pregnancy as a mere annoyance. The urgency of women's need to end unwanted pregnancy is measured by their willingness to risk death and mutilation, to spend huge sums of money, and to endure the indignities of illegal abortion. Women only have abortions when the alternative is unendurable. Women take both abortion and motherhood very seriously.

She had her fun, now let her pay for it. If you have sex, you should expect to get pregnant.

This vindictive, self-righteous attitude shows scorn for women. Motherhood should never be forced on women as a punishment for having sex, and no child should ever be born as a punishment for it's mother. Punishing the man is never mentioned...

Most unwanted pregnancies become wanted children. Women make mistakes having abortions.

Many unwanted children are abused, neglected and/or battered by unloving or immature parents. Some are killed or abandoned after birth by women who delivered alone. Many women make mistakes in having babies they don't want and can't love or care for.

There are alternatives to abortion. Abortion is never necessary.

A Carter administration study group on alternatives to

abortion disbanded after concluding that the only real alternatives are "suicide, motherhood, and, some would add, madness." No woman should be forced to bear a child only to give it up for adoption. Psychologically, giving up a child is far more traumatic than having an early abortion. Married couples find it impossible to give up unwanted children...

Abortion causes psychological damage to women.
The Institute of Medicine of the National Academy of Sciences has concluded that abortion is not associated with a detectable increase in the incidence of mental illness. The depression and guilt feelings reported by some women are usually mild, temporary and outweighed by feelings of relief. Women choosing abortion should be informed of the risks and benefits of the procedure and should decide for themselves what to do...

THE FREEDOM TO HAVE ABORTION

The issue is not merely whether the religious or moral beliefs of one group should be imposed on the entire population. That is oversimplification, for those who favor individual choice do not require all women to have abortions. Those who want the law to impose their beliefs, however, would require that none could have abortion, with prison as the penalty. Pro-abortionists want freedom to have — or reject — abortion. Anti-abortionists want to deny choice, forcing their standard on all.

The Milwaukee Journal, June 17, 1974.

There is a lack of adoptable babies because of abortion being legal.
Women should not be forced to have babies for infertile couples. Adoptable babies are also scarce because today 93% of unwed teenage mothers keep their babies. Though many thousands of children (older, non-white, handicapped) still wait in institutions and foster homes, the baby shortage has resulted in some couples adopting these hard-to-place children.

No woman should be allowed to have an abortion without the man's consent. It's his baby, too, and he should be able to stop the mother from killing it.

The Supreme Court ruled that the State may not give a man power to veto a woman's decision to abort. Even though such a conflict may be very sad for a man, the needs of the woman are overriding; she is the one who must bear the child and is usually the one who is responsible for its care.

Teens should not be allowed to have abortions without parental consent.

A parental consent requirement gives a parent the right to veto a daughter's decision to abort. The Supreme Court ruled that parental consent laws are unconstitutional.

Parents have the right and responsibility to guide their children in important decisions. A law requiring parental notification of a daughter's abortion would strengthen the family unit.

Many teenagers voluntarily consult their parents, but some

"Since the Supreme Court ruling, the phrase Freedom of Choice has been used to show support for keeping abortion safe, legal and available to all women."

Reprinted courtesy of National Abortion Rights Action League.

simply will not. Forcing the involvement of unsympathetic, authoritarian or very moralistic parents in a teen's pregnancy (and sexuality) can damage the family unit beyond repair. Some family units are already under so much stress that knowledge of an unwed pregnancy could be disastrous.

Pro-abortionists are anti-family. Abortion destroys the American family.

The unwanted child of a teenaged mother has little chance to grow up in a normal, happy American home. Instead, a new family is created: a child and her child, both destined for a life of poverty and hopelessness. Legal abortion helps women limit their families to the number of children they want and can afford, both emotionally and financially, and reduces the number of children born unwanted. Pro-choice is definitely pro-family.

Doctors violate the Hippocratic Oath by performing abortions. Doctors should preserve life, not destroy it.

The modern Oath contains nothing that can be construed as forbidding abortion. Most doctors are primarily concerned with the health of their patients, and want abortion to take place under optimum medical conditions. Doctors do not want the law to interfere with the exercise of their best medical judgment.

"I consider the deliberate taking of a human fetus from the body of a mother-to-be an act of violence."

Abortion Is An Act Of Violence

James P. Shannon

James P. Shannon is an attorney in Albuquerque, New Mexico and teaches at the University of New Mexico law school. A former Catholic priest and auxiliary bishop of St. Paul, Minnesota, he has published numerous articles in various Catholic publications. In the following viewpoint, Mr. Shannon reviews the Supreme Court abortion decision of 1973 and presents a view of abortion from the perspective of both the embryo and the mother.

Consider the following questions while reading:
1. What was the Supreme Court's decision in the case of Roe v. Wade on January 22, 1973?
2. Why does Mr. Shannon feel that abortion within three months of conception is not a morally neutral act?
3. What conclusion has Mr. Shannon reached as a result of counseling women who have had abortions?

From James P. Shannon's weekly column "The Pilgrim Church," *The Minneapolis Tribune*, February 18 and 25, 1973. Reprinted with permission from *The Minneapolis Tribune.*

Few decisions of the Supreme Court have ever been simultaneously praised and denounced as enthusiastically as that handed down by the court January 22, 1973, in the decision styled Roe vs. Wade. By a vote of 7 to 2, with Justices White and Rehnquist dissenting, the court struck down as unconstitutional any state law that denies a pregnant woman the right to an abortion during the first three months (first trimester) of her pregnancy.

Proponents of abortion have praised the Supreme Court for the wisdom and the courage of its decision. And right-to-life committees, organized in most states, have promptly announced plans to fight the Supreme Court decision by a massive campaign of political pressure, directed at the court, the Congress and the President. Saying that they speak for the human rights of the unborn, these committees are convinced that a human person exists in the womb of a mother from the moment of conception.

Writing for the majority of the court in Roe, Justice Blackmun says: "We need not resolve the difficult question of when life begins. When those trained in the respective disciplines of medicine, philosophy and theology are unable to arrive at any consensus, the judiciary, at this point in the development of man's knowledge, is not in a position to speculate as to the answer."

WHEN LIFE BEGINS

Critics of the majority opinion quickly respond that the question of when life begins in the human fetus is precisely the critical question and that it cannot be side-stepped by the court simply by admitting that it is a tough question.

Writing in dissent for the minority, Justice White said: "I find nothing in the language or history of the Constitution to support the court's judgment. The court simply fashions and announces a new constitutional right for pregnant mothers and, with scarcely any reason or authority for its action, invests that right with sufficient substance to override most existing state abortion statutes."

It is worth noting that the opinion of the majority spends an unusually large amount of space discussing the medical, ethical and legislative history of deliberate abortion. It almost seems that the majority rests its case on a lack of consensus among professionals in disciplines outside the law and then proceeds to build on this shaky foundation in new principles of law.

I would defend, without endorsing, the majority opinion on the ground that both sides in this perennial debate ultimately rest their case on premises of belief that neither one can prove scientifically or with finality.

The pro-abortionists believe that the human fetus is not a human person (in the sense that the term is used in the 14th Amendment) until it is capable of living outside the womb.

The anti-abortionists believe that the human fetus, from the moment of conception, is indeed a human person, with all the constitutional rights assured to other human persons. I confess that I share this opinion.

It seems to me as clear as daylight that abortion would be a crime.

Mahatma Gandhi

I do admit, however, that it is an opinion. I think I can give several reasonable arguments in support of it. However, to share this fundamental belief with other persons does not mean that I endorse the current political campaigns to amend the Constitution, to reprove the Supreme Court or to devise new state laws prohibiting abortion.

Quite the contrary. I have said more than once, and I now repeat the opinion, that the decision to perform an abortion should be a moral and medical judgment made in good conscience by a pregnant woman and her doctor.

A VIOLATION OF NATURE

To say that is certainly not to endorse the concept of "abortion on demand." In fact, I consider the deliberate taking of a human fetus from the body of a mother-to-be an act of violence. It seems to me to be a deliberate violation of nature, even though I admit there are circumstances in which it might be justified.

I believe that one fuzzy conclusion reached by many pro-abortionists who read the Supreme Court decision carelessly is that deliberate abortion within three months of conception is simply a morally neutral act. I would argue that the fetus, whether person or non-person at that time, has an identity, integrity, sacredness and potentiality which should not be promiscuously abused or denied.

Editorializing in the Christian Century, J. Claude Evans urges that "pro-abortionists and anti-abortionists...unite on taking the matter of abortion out of the statute books altogether." Although my premises are not precisely those of Evans, I find it easily possible to concur wholeheartedly in the reasonableness of his final proposal on abortion.

These are his words: "About all we need on the statute book is some limiting law — perhaps stating that no abortions are permitted beyond 18-week gestation and protecting the right of any doctor or hospital to refuse to perform abortions on demand. The effect of the destatutizing of abortion would be to show respect for the pluralism of our society. Anti-abortionist individuals and churches would be free to teach their faith views without the onus of a permissive state law that would make their teaching more difficult.

"At the same time, pro-abortionists would also be able to teach their faith views without the support of a state law that would tend to give them the illusion of universality. And the ecumenical community would find itself enriched by the seriousness of communally apprehended standards without leaning on the state to do its dirty work of moral enforcement."

I say "amen" to the Evans proposal...

ABORTION FROM THE EMBRYO'S POINT OF VIEW

Look at the question from the point of view of the human embryo. It is a human embryo from the moment the female ovum is fertilized. Allowed to grow to term, it will be a small but fully human person at birth. Its life from conception is a growing continuum. And conversely, if that spark of life be ended before birth, the living entity that ends is more than merely an appendage to the body of the mother.

The Supreme Court...decided that it is now permissible under the law for a pregnant woman and her doctor to terminate life in the womb between the time of conception

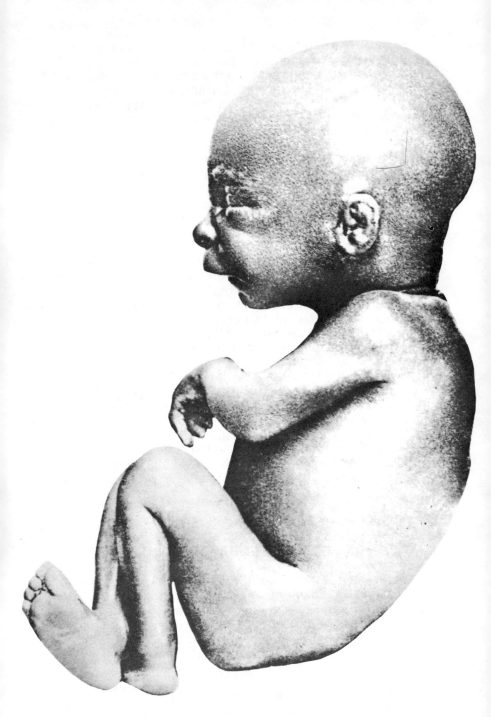

Unborn baby at 20 weeks. Actual size.

and a date six months later.

A close reading of the court's opinion would seem to say that the human fetus cannot be taken from the mother in the last trimester (three months) of pregnancy, except for certain grave reasons, can readily be taken in the first trimester, and can, under specified conditions, be taken during the middle three months of pregnancy.

Apart from the arithmetical symmetry of those three neat periods of gestation, one seeks in vain in the court's opinion for any substantive reason why the legal rights inhering in the human fetus change quality after 90 days and again after 180 days. What accounts for these changes? And who decides that these changes are sufficient to permit or to ban abortion?

The simple answer for us now is that the Supreme Court has decided. And on what premise? We do not know. Seven of nine justices have declared that what is permissible for six months after conception may be criminally illegal thereafter. And under the law of this nation, that question is settled for the present. It is settled, however, only in the sense that the Supreme Court is, under the Constitution, the final arbiter of the law in our legal system.

If human life is sacred in hospital wards and nurseries, if it is sacred in Death Row at San Quentin and if it is sacred in rest homes for the infirm and elderly, then it must be sacred wherever it exists, inside or outside the womb. Human life is human life from its beginning to its ending.

ABORTION FROM THE MOTHER'S POINT OF VIEW

Consider abortion from the point of view of the mother-to-be. Why, in a given instance, does she wish to terminate her pregnancy? Because she was raped? Because her child may be born deformed? Because she already has too many children? Because she regrets the occasion of conception? Because she cannot psychologically or economically bear the burden of rearing another child?

Each of these reasons, and a host of others, merits careful weighing. Each deserves to be balanced in the scales against the rights that inhere in the unborn human fetus.

If the right to life is sacred, then the right of an unborn child to be born and to grow and to develop his potentialities deserves, at the very least, to be balanced against the psycho-

James P. Shannon

logical, physical, human and economic needs of his mother and family-to-be.

In the current round of public discussion of abortion, many women who are prominent in society have publicly acknowledged that they have obtained abortions recently. They do not argue that they were raped or that they feared their babies would be born deformed. They candidly admit that they got pregnant when they did not wish to do so. Is that a good enough reason for ending the pregnancy? I say it is not.

If a woman believes that her right to control her own body extends always and easily to the violent act of abortion, I respectfully submit that her concern for the integrity of her body should begin at least 91 days before the end of her first trimester of pregnancy...

TRAUMATIC CONSEQUENCES OF ABORTION

My experience in counseling women who have had abortions, both legally and illegally, leads me to the conclusion that the burdens of bearing a baby to term, even an unwanted or unexpected baby, which is later put up for adoption, are usually far less traumatic than the consequences of deliberate abortion.

I am aware that many regular readers will disagree vehemently with the thesis and the premises for this column. I do not mean to say either that such persons are wrong or that I am right.

I merely offer today, out of "a decent respect for the opinion of mankind," some reasons that impel me to believe that abortion is an act of violence and therefore not to be taken lightly in any culture that still professes to base its legal and ethical system on the premise that all human life is sacred.

CASE STUDY:
FETAL
EXPERIMENTATION

The picture below shows a British doctor at Cambridge University's Department of Experimental Medicine experimenting on a living, legally aborted human fetus. The doctor explains that he is "using something which is destined for the incinerator to benefit mankind."

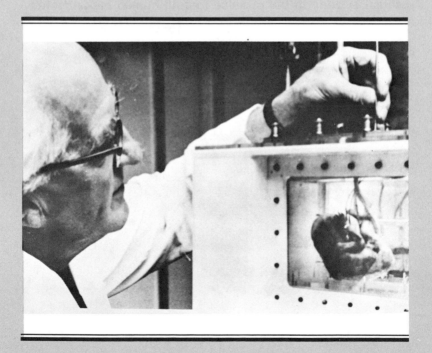

INSTRUCTIONS

Your state legislature is debating a bill that would permit experimentation on aborted fetuses until the 28th week of pregnancy.

STEP 1. The class should break into groups of four to six students.

STEP 2. Each group should pretend it represents a church council with the problem of deciding what position to take on the issue for the purpose of influencing its state senator.

STEP 3. After a majority of the members of each council decide what position to take, the council should be able to present its reasoning to the whole class.

ARGUMENTS FOR FETAL EXPERIMENTATION

1. The fetus has no personality and feelings, and need not be accorded the rights of a human being.
2. Experimentation would benefit all mankind and lessen the suffering of many.
3. One cannot stop the march of progess.

ARGUMENTS AGAINST FETAL EXPERIMENTATION

1. The fetus should be granted the rights due other human persons.
2. Fetal experimentation is worse than murder, and can be compared to torture before execution.
3. Abortion is the best alternative between two negative choices; it should not be worsened by fetal experimentation.

"A civilized society does not condone the killing of its young."

The Case For Pro-Life

David LaFontaine

David LaFontaine is active in politics in Minnesota and has written several guest columns in the *Minneapolis Star* on political affairs and social justice issues. In the following viewpoint, Mr. LaFontaine answers the critics of the Pro-Life movement and defends the movement's attempt to ban abortion through legislative action.

Consider the following questions while reading:
1. **What three points does the author address in defending his pro-life position?**
2. **How does the author relate society's treatment of its young to the treatment it gives to older citizens?**
3. **Why does the author think a constitutional amendment is the solution to the abortion situation? Do you agree?**

David LaFontaine, "Pro-life: Some Answers for the Critics," *The Minneapolis Star*, January 31, 1980. Reprinted by permission of the author.

On January 22, 1973, the United States Supreme Court ruled that the states may not legislate with regard to abortion during the first 12 weeks after conception. The court further ruled that the states may, in limited fashion, legislate on this subject after 12 weeks. That limitation prohibits states from enacting an outright ban on abortions.

Following is an overview of the right-to-life position that covers the following points: 1) Why we are opposed to abortion, 2) why we consider it proper to implement our position through the legislative process, and 3) principal criticisms of our position answered.

Hubert Humphrey said that we may judge a society by the way in which it treats its very old and its very young. Cultures that have appeared primitive to the modern Western mind have been known to respect their elders as the repository of wisdom. Many of them have also been highly protective of their young as being the hope of the future.

We view with growing alarm the way in which our culture treats these two groups. We have chosen to speak for those most helpless members of society who cannot speak for themselves — the unborn.

WHY WE ARE OPPOSED TO ABORTION

What takes place during an abortion?: Euphemisms aside, we have a very small person who is destroyed in any one of a number of unpleasant ways. If you find this thought disturbing, consider the discomfort of the victims.

Modern science leaves no doubt that the human person exists at conception. We know, therefore, that an induced abortion, for whatever reason, destroys a human life.

Abortion proponents contend that under certain circumstances abortion is a merciful alternative to an otherwise wretched life. They refer to physical deformity, extreme poverty, and the likelihood of severe child abuse. This argument confuses the quality of life with life itself.

We reply that man has no authority to destroy life once it has begun. Man does not have the right to determine whose life is not worth living.

Further, the great majority of abortions are sought not for medical reasons, not because of financial problems, not through fear of a deformed child, but simply because the woman does not want to be pregnant. The great majority of abortions are obtained not out of considerations of crises but of convenience.

The National Organization for Women claims that the decision to abort is properly the right of the woman to make. We do not agree. In deciding to terminate her pregnancy, a woman is also deciding to terminate a life. While the Supreme Court has determined that a woman may legally kill her unborn child, we believe that she has never had this right as an absolute, does not have it now, and cannot be granted such a right by any civil authority.

A civilized society does not condone the killing of its young. To do so marks it as a society built upon a foundation of the basest form of utilitarianism. It is one thing to evaluate technological achievements on the basis of their material return in pleasure or usefulness. It is quite another to so judge human beings who have an intrinsic value of their own.

Our generation applies the term barbarian to a society that accepted the legal killing of 6 million Jews in 12 years. As this is written, our society has accepted the legal killing of a far greater number of children in only seven.

ABORTION IS THREAT TO SOCIETY

"To destroy human life, which has already begun, is a threat to all humanity. The basis of a free society is fundamentally rooted in the concept that violence to one is a menace to all."

Bishop Daniel P. Reilly, *Catholic Twin Circle*, May 17, 1981.

Since 1973, legalized abortion has been the "law of the land." Therefore, claim abortion advocates, the issue has been settled and is no longer an appropriate subject for public debate.

Not exactly.

The court has circumscribed the legal term "person." Some years back, the court included corporate entities in this category. In 1973 it absolutely excluded fetal life before viability. We consider such a reversal of priority to be an insult to basic human dignity. For that reason we seek a constitutional amendment that will give unborn children the same standing before the law as any state-chartered corporation.

USING THE LEGISLATIVE PROCESS

Just as honorable citizens refused to let the Dred Scott decision remain the law of the land, so do we seek to change what we believe to be an unjust law. Just as women have made vigorous use of the legal process to attain what they consider their moral and/or human rights, so do we seek what we believe to be the moral and human rights of unborn children.

The Constitution of the United States is a magnificent document. It was developed and adopted by high-minded, intelligent and articulate people. They wisely provided for its change through a process that discourages frivolous attachments. Many groups have availed themselves of this process. We see no reason to be hesitant about using the amendment function in the interests of so vital a cause as human life.

The Declaration of Independence states that among mankind's inalienable rights is the right to life. Since 1973 that right has been in serious jeopardy. We seek to have the Constitution guarantee what the Declaration of Independence proclaimed.

ANSWERS TO CRITICISM

No one is forced to have an abortion. Not yet. A professor at the University of Chicago would allow each woman credits equivalent to 2.3 children. Should she wish more she would have to purchase additional credits from a woman not desiring her "share." Should a woman have more than the allotted number of children, she would be sterilized, forcibly if necessary. We have every expectation that mandatory abortion under certain circumstances will be advocated in the near future by supposedly responsible groups or individuals.

We should not attempt to impose our morality on others. Society imposes the morality of the majority each time a legislature meets. Abortion advocates would impose *their* morality on *us* by requiring that our tax dollars be used to fund abortions.

Our case is based on the tenets of the Roman Catholic Church and thus violates First Amendment dicta on separation of church and state. No one denies that the Catholic Church opposes abortion. Indeed, Catholics ought to take great pride in that position. No one denies that abortion is an issue about which many Catholics share deep concern. It is manifestly not true that the Catholic Church is the only spiritual institution opposing abortion in the United States. It is not the only Catholic issue. Neither is it only a Catholic issue.

Catholics in the right–to–life movement face a double standard. In the 1960s, the church was in the forefront of two highly controversial issues. Catholics, from bishops to lay people, vigorously opposed the Vietnam War. Catholic priests went to jail for their participation in anti-war activities. At that time there were no anguished calls for church/state separation from those who now protest Catholic involvement in the abortion issue. The Catholic Church was deeply involved in the civil rights struggle during the same period. At that time, the only complaint from these same people regarding Catholic participation was that it was too little and too late. Those who now seek to order Catholics out of the abortion issue by using church/state separation arguments do so in bad faith.

Reprinted by permission of *The Wanderer*.

We are guilty of bad taste when we publish pictures of aborted babies. It was perfectly proper to use pictures out of Vietnam that sickened anyone with a shred of human feeling. The same may be said of Auschwitz and Wounded Knee. We believe that we are fully justified in bringing home to as many people as possible the reality of what happens in an abortion. To the extent that those pictures disturb their views, they perform exactly the function they are intended to perform. A reform movement, to be effective, must illustrate in a forceful manner those conditions it wishes to correct.

Anti-abortion activists have engaged in violence against property, as well as persons. Responsible participants in our cause have deplored and will continue to deplore violence of any kind. We oppose the burning of abortion clinics in 1980 just as we opposed the bombing of public buildings 12 years ago.

Abortion should not be a political issue. Any issue of public policy on which large numbers of citizens disagree becomes, by definition, a political issue. It will continue to be so until an accomodation acceptable to major segments of both sides is reached.

We would force maternity but we abandon the woman in her time of distress. Our movement includes organizations that provide psychological and material aid to women faced with problem pregnancies. We regard it as an obligation of society to give every needed assistance to women in such circumstances. We do not view pregnancy as a punishment for sin but as an opportunity to offer the gift of life to another human being. We hold that a truly civilized society, rather than telling a woman to destroy her child, will come to her aid and treat her with dignity and compassion.

We are responsive when confronted with the claims of those less fortunate. Otherwise we would favor abortion as more economical than raising a child at public expense — an argument that our opponents frequently use. The solution to the problem of the poor does not lie in their extermination, Garret Hardin notwithstanding.

Population considerations demand a liberal abortion policy. Are those who make this claim really concerned about scarcity or are they apprehensive about sharing the resources of this earth? In the United States we comprise 6 percent of the world's population. We consume 30 percent of the world's resources. This is a shameful statistic. We only

David LaFontaine

add to that shame by urging that more of the world's poor be the victims of genocide so as not to disturb that imbalance.

An abortion ban will mean a return of back alley butchers for most women while those of means will simply go out of the country. Abortion butchery, far from being curtailed by the Supreme Court decision, has merely been given legal approval. Investigative reporting in 1978 by the Chicago Sun-Times documented, among other practices, fraudulent abortions performed on women who were not pregnant, grossly unsanitary conditions, haphazard procedures leading to permanent physical damage and death, falsification of records, and abortions performed by doctors while under the influence of alcohol.

We are confronted by a society that tells a woman that she may kill her unborn child for any reason or for no reason. We insist that a more humane social policy would be to provide a compassionate atmosphere that says to a woman, "We care for you. We care for your child. Together let us provide every possible opportunity for you and this new life to reach your maximum potential. With a loving concern it can be done." Idealistic? Of course it is. Civilization advances through such ideals. It withers without them.

"Supporters of safe, legal abortion do indeed respect life. So much, in fact, that we believe medically supervised care should be available to women who conclude that an unwanted pregnancy must not continue."

The Case For Pro-Choice

Betty Benjamin

Betty Benjamin, president of the Abortion Rights Council of Minnesota, is married and the mother of three. She is on the board of directors of Family and Children Service, is the past president of Unity Settlement Association and is active in church affairs. In the following viewpoint, Mrs. Benjamin argues that pro-choice supporters are not necessarily pro-abortion but rather support the rights of individuals to freedom of conscience and access to quality medical care.

Consider the following question while reading:
1. **What does the author mean when she says "we are not pro-abortion"?**
2. **What point does the author make after asking the question "Who should control reproduction, the individual or the government?"**
3. **What charges does the author level at the anti-abortion lobby?**

Betty Benjamin, "Pro-choice: Keep Abortion a Private Matter," *The Minneapolis Star*, January 31, 1980. Reprinted by permission of the author.

The majority of the American people are being told that they do not respect life. Those are the charges hurled by the anti-abortion lobby, the so-called "pro-life" movement.

Members of the Abortion Rights Council of Minnesota, along with at least two-thirds of all Americans, believe that abortion is a private matter and should be available to all women.

WE RESPECT LIFE

Supporters of safe, legal abortions do indeed respect life. So much, in fact, that we believe medically supervised care should be available to women who conclude that an unwanted pregnancy must not continue.

We are not "pro-abortion," a fact that our critics are unable to grasp. We support the right of every individual to freedom of conscience in matters of reproductive choices and access to good quality medical care, including the provision of abortion services, for all women.

There are occasional failures with all methods of birth control. People fail, too, for that matter. Unfortunately, not everyone is knowledgeable, careful or sexually responsible at all times.

Nor does every woman or girl have sufficiently good health to safely carry a pregnancy to term. What are we to say to her? Take your chances? Or do we provide her with the professional care and medical options her condition requires?

To some, long-held moral values are threatened by what they view as a "permissive" attitude toward sexuality. The unstated message of their opposition to abortion is that sexual relations for anything but procreation should be "punished."

The Abortion Rights Council does not agree that retribution or punishment for women with problem pregnancies would change behavior. A humanitarian, compassionate approach assists people in planning for better futures.

The world is already burdened with an overabundance of social problems stemming from the high rates of birth of unwanted children. In poor families, it is one of the perpetuating causes of poverty.

Betty Benjamin

Among the 800,000 unplanned, unwanted children born every year in the U.S., many become loved and wanted. Unfortunately, many others end up as battered children, delinquents, and criminals. Studies of battered children reveal a high percentage of unmarried and unwanted pregnancy, or forced marriage among the abusive parents.

Public opinion polls reveal that 60–88 percent of people in this country think abortion should be legal either in all or some circumstances. And most (79 percent) are worried by efforts of a small but powerful minority to dictate to the rest of us how we should live. Of Catholics questioned in a June, 1979, Gallup Poll, 21 percent agreed that abortion should be legal under *all* circumstances. An additional 52 percent agreed that abortion should be legal "under certain circumstances."

Most Americans do not want to impose their religious and moral beliefs on others. Many are angered by the Khomeini-like absolutism of the anti-abortion faction that does not allow for differences in the deepest-held personal beliefs of fellow Americans.

Twenty-eight national religious organizations, representing 15 major denominations, banded together in 1974 as the Religious Coalition for Abortion Rights (RCAR), "to safeguard legal abortion on the basis of faith and moral conviction." The coalition, an educational group, represents Methodist, Presbyterian, Baptist, Episcopal, and Jewish groups, as well as Catholic laity and a few clergy (Catholics for a Free Choice).

The major question is one of *control:* Who should control reproduction, the individual or the government?

INDIVIDUAL CONTROL OF LIFE

The U.S. Supreme Court decisions of Jan. 22, 1973, focused most attention on this controversy. But the decisions had nothing to do with "abortion on demand," the code word and slogan of the anti-abortion lobby. The 1973 case, Roe vs. Wade, supported the right to privacy and proper medical care for women seeking abortion services. That opinion affirmed that abortion is a private decision between a woman and her physician.

The Supreme Court found no compelling government interest in *forcing* women to remain pregnant during the early months of pregnancy. Simple justice in an egalitarian society requires that women be permitted personal decisions regarding problem pregnancies...

Contrary to the false statements of those opposing all abortions, this procedure is at least eight times safer for the woman than a full-term pregnancy and delivery. In 1974, a year after the Supreme Court decision, the number of deaths from abortion dropped by a dramatic 40 percent, primarily because the procedure had become legal and performed by qualified doctors. The drop in the death rate reflected the decline in the number of illegal abortions performed in this nation, from a high of one million per year...

THE BEGINNING OF LIFE

Since life itself is a continuum, to argue about precisely "when life begins" during fetal development is to pursue an exercise in futility. Opponents of abortion base their case upon the premise that personhood begins when sperm meets egg. Rather, in the true scientific sense, an embryo or fetus is comparable to a set of blueprints up to the state of independent viability. The fetus becomes less primordial and more human-like with every week of development. At what exact moment is it so human that it should be granted legal protection? The answer to this question varies from person to person, depending primarily upon one's personal philosophy and religious faith.

Reprinted by courtesy of the *Fort Worth Star-Telegram*.

Most of us have seen photographs of a 16–week–old fetus showing development with breath–taking clarity and beauty. We have been stirred by this close look at beginnings of our own kind. But is a fertilized egg really a human being, or does it harbor only the *potential* of one? Is a one–ounce fetus a person, the same as you and I? This is the size, at 12 weeks, at which almost 90 percent of all abortions have been completed.

Those who oppose abortion argue for the rights of the fetus. One must respect their right, in their own personal lives, to view the fetus as equal in value to the pregnant woman. Equal respect should be given to those of us who consider the life, welfare, and needs of the pregnant woman of ultimately greater importance in the decision whether to continue pregnancy.

Theological discussions of when life begins reflect the world's diverse religious views. Some believe that human life begins when the fetus stirs, at "quickening." (That, in fact, was the teaching of the Roman Catholic Church for centuries.) Others believe that significant life does not come until birth. Teachings on the matter have varied throughout history.

Should our laws reflect only the views of those theologies that teach that a *person* exists from the moment the egg and sperm unite?

A POLITICAL ISSUE

What should be a personal decision has become a *political* issue. With an evangelical fervor and single-mindedness, those wanting to remove abortion as an option are seeking a "human life" amendment to the United States Constitution or the advocating of a constitutional convention to outlaw *all* abortion. Besides overriding the rights of the majority of Americans who favor abortion, birth control, and sex education as needed services, this action would have legal consequences that could well threaten the survival of our democracy itself.

A "human life" amendment would give the fertilized egg the same rights of persons already born. It would make abortion more restrictive than at any time in our history.

It would make a woman having an abortion, for whatever reason, and doctors performing them, murderers. A woman with a miscarriage might have to prove it was not self-induced.

Because certain oral contraceptives and the intrauterine (IUD) ring prevent a fertilized egg from implanting itself on the walls of the uterus, users of these contraceptives would be guilty of murder.

And, of course, abortions would continue — a fact anti-abortion spokespersons do not deny. Abortions would still be available in illegal, unsafe places just as they were before 1973.

A constitutional convention is even more risky to contemplate. There are no precedents or guidelines by which to structure it. Legal experts warn that there is absolutely no way of limiting such a convention to any single issue. Yet, 19 states have already called for such a convention.

THE ANTI-ABORTION MOVEMENT

Spearheading the anti-abortion movement is the hierarchy of the Roman Catholic Church. The church structure and money make possible much of the anti-abortion activity across the country, even though only 24 percent of its own members think all abortion should be outlawed.

Political allies of the anti-abortion movement, generally the fundamentalist churches, along with the Mormon Church, have been joined by the "New Right," a movement preying on the fears of single-issue groups for support. It is not coincidence that the "hit list" of 12 members of Congress targeted for defeat in 1980 by the Life Amendment Political Action Committee was identical with those of the "New Right."

According to several speakers at a conference on the "New Right" held recently in Minneapolis, abortion is the focal issue of the "New Right."

Those in the anti-abortion movement use inflammatory statements. They try to scare women. They claim legal abortion is very hazardous. In fact, it is safer than childbearing or tonsillectomy. They say that legal abortion will jeopardize future childbearing. In fact, research has demonstrated future childbearing is not adversely affected. They say that pregnancy after rape is "extremely rare" when, in fact, 3 percent of the victims become pregnant.

The anti-abortion lobby, with distortions and often with no documentation, distributes photographs of large, bloody fetuses from rare, late abortions, hoping the public will believe this is typical abortion practice. The Abortion Rights Council has until now resisted countering with photos of bloody women killed by illegal abortions or photos of unwanted, abandoned new-borns left to die.

But even more frustrating is the semantic battle that is going on. Pregnant women are designated as "mothers." Self-identified as "pro-life" abortion opponents are strangely preoccupied with the fetus. To them every fertilized egg is a healthy, frollicking baby. They exhibit no more than rhetoric in their caring about women and their families. They work

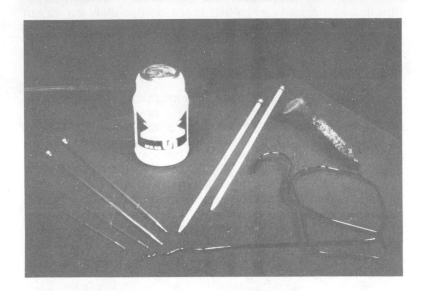

"Estimates in the late 1960's indicated as many as one million illegal abortions a year for American women. Poor women had to resort to crude methods of self-abortion, risking infection and injury."

Reprinted courtesy of National Abortion Rights Action League.

against birth control programs and against sex education offerings in the schools.

The punitive approach of abortion opponents and their political candidates floods over into other areas, such as equal rights for women, nutrition and education assistance programs for poor children, and capital punishment.

The Abortion Rights Council cares about these issues. We are convinced such programs could help reduce the number of abortions in this country. You would think those who are opposed to abortion would be in the front lines helping us *prevent* unwanted pregnancies. We challenge them to state what *constructive* steps their movement is taking to reduce the need for abortion. Making it illegal is *not* a constructive step.

DISTINGUISHING BETWEEN FACT AND OPINION

This discussion activity is designed to promote experimentation with one's ability to distinguish between fact and opinion. It is a fact, for example, that the United States was militarily involved in the Vietnam War. But to say this involvement served the interests of world peace is an opinion or conclusion. Future historians will agree that American soldiers fought in Vietnam, but their interpretations about the causes and consequences of the war will probably vary greatly.

PART I

Instructions

Many of the following statements are taken from the viewpoints in this book; some have other origins. Consider each statement carefully. Mark (O) for any statement you feel is an opinion or interpretation of the facts. Mark (F) for any statement you believe is a fact. Discuss and compare your judgments with those of other class members.

O = Opinion
F = Fact

_____ 1. Abortion violates the God-given natural law.

_____ 2. The movement for abortion on demand is a symptom of a selfish society.

_____ 3. Abortion is an effective method of limiting population.

_____ 4. The human fetus does not become a human person until after birth.

_____ 5. The unborn fetus deserves the same care we give the retarded and other handicapped individuals in our society.

_____ 6. Abortions are more easily obtained by wealthy women.

_____ 7. The decision to abort is often the best choice one can make between available alternatives in an imperfect world.

_____ 8. Rape should be sufficient reason to abort, regardless of the age of the fetus.

_____ 9. Any state law that denies a pregnant woman an abortion during the first three months of her pregnancy is unconstitutional.

_____ 10. Abortion is the first step to the complete disregard for life that was characteristic of Nazi Germany.

_____ 11. Carrying an unwanted baby to term is less traumatic for the mother than the consequences of deliberate abortion.

_____ 12. In the U.S., abortions may be legally performed at any time before birth under certain circumstances.

_____ 13. Men, not women, in the Western world, have traditionally made the decision of whether or not to abort.

_____ 14. No woman should be forced to have a child she does not want.

PART II

Instructions

STEP 1. The class should break into groups of four to six students.

STEP 2. Each small group should try to locate two statements of fact and two statements of opinion in the book. First examine viewpoints five and six in this chapter and then turn to other viewpoints if necessary.

STEP 3. Each group should choose a student to record its statements.

STEP 4. The whole class should discuss and compare the small groups' results.

BIBLIOGRAPHY

The following list of periodical articles deals with the subject matter of this chapter.

W.F. Buckley — *Right to Life Breakthrough,* **National Review,** March 20, 1981, p. 313.

Charles DeCelles — *Conservatives and Liberals on Prolife Issues,* **America,** May 2, 1981, p. 365.

E.R. Dobell — *Abortion: The Controversy We Can't Seem to Solve,* **Redbook,** June, 1979, p.42.

R.B. Gratz — *Never Again! Never Again? Can We Lose Our Right to Abortion?,* **Ms,** July, 1977, p. 54.

C. Hartshorne — *Concerning Abortion: An Attempt At a Rational View,* **The Christian Century,** January 21, 1981, p. 42.

Humanist — *Free Choice,* January/February, 1981, p. 101.

W. Isaacson — *Battle Over Abortion,* **Time,** April 6, 1981, p. 88.

J. Krastel — *Return to Realism: A Prolife Agenda,* **America,** February 7, 1981, p. 101.

E.J. McMahon — *Why a Constitutional Convention is Needed: Human Life Amendment,* **America,** July 2, 1977, p. 12.

M. Meehan — *Abortion: The Left Has Betrayed the Sanctity of Life,* **The Progressive,** September, 1980, p. 32.

P. Metsky — *Man's View on Abortion,* **Glamour,** January, 1981, p. 150.

Nation — *Legislating Life,* March 28, 1981, p. 355.

A. Neier — *To Deal With the Right to Life Forces,* **Current,** January, 1981, p. 29.

R.J. Neuhaus — *Hyde and Hysteria,* **The Christian Century,** September 10–17, 1980, p. 849.

C. Poston and E. Morgan — *Abortion Rights,* **Humanist,** September/October, 1980, p. 42.

G. Steinem — *Nazi Connection,* **Ms,** October, 1980, p. 88.

M. Stucky — *Abortion Harassment,* **McCalls,** March, 1979, p. 52.

Time — *The Battle Over Abortion,* April 6, 1981, p. 22.

R.M. Williams — *Power of Fetal Politics: Anti-Abortion Groups,* **Saturday Review,** June 9, 1979, p. 12.

Chapter 3

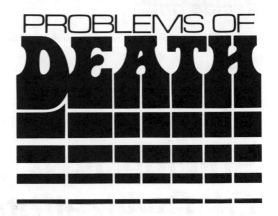

PROBLEMS OF DEATH

Is Suicide Ever Justified?

"Someday we may praise people who meet death on their own terms — at the time, place, and manner they decide on."

Suicide Is A Sign Of Civilization

Herbert A. Tonne

Herbert A. Tonne is professor emeritus at the State University of New York at Albany and a former member of the American Humanist Association's board of directors. In the following viewpoint, Mr. Tonne argues that suicide should be given a status similar to euthanasia and, in fact, makes reference to suicide as "autoeuthanasia."

Consider the following questions while reading:
1. What historical basis does Mr. Tonne offer for acceptance of suicide?
2. According to Mr. Tonne, what are some of the causes of suicide among youth?
3. On what "fundamental right" does Mr. Tonne base his acceptance of suicide?

Herbert A. Tonne, "Suicide: Is It Autoeuthanasia?" This article first appeared in *The Humanist* July/August 1979 and is reprinted by permission.

Albert Camus said that the decision to commit suicide is the only basic philosophical question. Camus may have exaggerated. But in terms of our increasing longevity and the ills accompanying it, suicide becomes a prime issue, one that is germane to our personal rights and liberties.

There is an increasing concern with death and dying. Some theorizers are still projecting the notion that there is a proper way to die and that the omission of any of the conventional stages in the process results in an improper death. In consideration of these trends, shouldn't we discuss the right of the individual to hasten death and avoid the pain of the concluding steps? We have lost our squeamishness about many other human acts. Why not, then, honestly analyze the morality of particular situations that might make suicide an act of reason and recognize its worthiness? In other words, I suggest that we call suicide autoeuthanasia.

SUICIDE AND CIVILIZATION

In imperial Rome suicide was honorable. Certain groups of Stoics and some Epicureans recommended it as an·alternative to the emptiness of life. Socrates preferred poison to exile. Prior to 1918, in Europe, suicide was a way to redeem oneself from class disgrace. Isn't it possible that as we grow more civilized the number of people who commit suicide will increase? We can already see a rough relationship between countries we regard as advanced and those with a high suicide rate. Havelock Ellis wrote, "Suicide without doubt is a test of height in civilization; it means that the population is winding up its nervous and intellectual system to the utmost point of tension and that sometimes it snaps."

Many of us know what it means to offer life a hostage. Those of us without close ties can justify a decision to end life. For those who have dependents, especially young children, the situation is different. They have accepted responsibilities; they have a social contract to fulfill.

Among better–educated young people suicide is a major cause of death. Since curiosity is one of our basic human urges, I would expect that youth would welcome what is ahead: Will we solve the employment problem? Will we have nuclear war? How will our sex lives change? Will space travel be for everyone? How will we develop new sources of energy? What changes will occur in our biological composition? What music, art, and literature will be produced?

I must admit that I am interested — nosy, if you will — and regret that I will not know the outcome of most of these questions. In a small way I envy the young man who will live to the year 2035. By then these problems will have been substantially altered, if not solved.

I often wonder why young people sometimes lack the courage to face life as past generations have. Perhaps some of the blame for "copping out" may be placed on the young people themselves. And, perhaps, some of the blame falls on the society-at-large. Breakdown of family life, unemployment, fear and hate of war, boredom, and the unwillingness of adults to acknowledge that young people grow up are some of the causes of suicide among youth. The proportion of men to women calling it quits, although still higher, is not as great as it was. Apparently equality between the sexes is even becoming evident in the refusal to face the meaninglessness of life. The incongruities of our civilization obviously affect young people. Our generation needs to be understanding.

DRINKING THE HEMLOCK

We do wish we might help to bring about a change in public opinion so that it would be recognized as honorable and proper for a person who has done a good life's work and is honestly weary from the burden, to so signify. We feel that after mature consideration, such a one should be allowed to drink the hemlock in some dignified and simple way.

Lucy Griscom Morgan, *Hastings Center Report.*

SINCERE AND PSEUDO-ATTEMPTS

Pseudo-attempts at suicide are often efforts to draw attention to real or imagined plights. Some individuals miscalculate and die. How many die accidentally? Or how many deaths attributed to other causes are suicide? Except as recorded on police blotters, statistics are not only vague, they are often falsified.

It does not matter whether people act sincerely or to win

attention, we should treat them with consideration. Fortunately there are social agencies that are ready to help either directly or indirectly. At least we have grown more tolerant than our ancestors, who viewed an attempt at suicide as a criminal act.

Relatives and friends are sometimes confused about the cause of a suicide. They may feel that they were at fault. A note of explanation is due them. Motion picture actor George Sanders understood this. Five tubes of nembutal lay next to his body along with a note that read: "Dear World, I am leaving you with the worries of this sweet cesspool — Good luck!" Sanders was sixty-five. While admiring his nonchalance, one cannot help quarreling with his cynicism. One would expect his native curiosity to have sustained him, that he would have perceived the social good he could have rendered to his fellow humans. Apart from the repugnance some may feel, I respect Sanders for doing what his reason dictated.

Some people who could be expected to accept the right to suicide oppose it. Schopenhauer said that suicide was a negation of the will. (In my view, when an individual wills his self-destruction, it may be fulfillment of the will.) Less vigorously, but for practically the same reason, Camus questioned suicide. Wittgenstein, who contemplated suicide often in his youth, finally regarded it as the ultimate sin...

Most liberals, and those who consider themselves apart from tradition, favor qualified euthanasia...One difficulty is that the practice of euthanasia can be easily abused. We become judges of the wishes of those for whom we act. Several times, I have been through the experience of being with people who died in pain. As I look back I wonder whether I should have taken positive action. It would have been difficult. More important, I am convinced that each one would have objected. To have acted only on my awareness would have been to take on the functions of deity. But not having acted has left me with the feeling that I did not have the courage to do what might have been best.

AUTOEUTHANASIA

Why limit ourselves to euthanasia? Why not go to the logical step of granting suicide the acceptance we give euthanasia and conceive of suicide as autoeuthanasia? Clearly, in this serious decision, freedom of action is justified. The right to make a decision for oneself is a fundamental right. A physician who has attended many cancer-ridden patients has told me that almost no one, knowing that the drugs at their bedside would give them surcease, uses them. We can ask: To what extent did they know? To what extent did they have the ability to take the drug? If a person wishes to continue to the bitter end, that should be his right. At the same time, isn't it equally right to call it quits and to avoid the suffering and degradation that is so often a prelude to death?

SUICIDE IS A SIGN OF FREEDOM

The full circle is being drawn. In classical times suicide was a tragic option, for human dignity's sake. Then for centuries it was a sin. Then it became a crime. Then a sickness. Soon it will become a choice again. Suicide is the signature of freedom.

Joseph Fletcher, *Humanhood: Essays in Biomedical Ethics.*

I would not refuse this right to anyone. Do we deny anyone the use of an automobile even though it kills fifty thousand people a year in the United States and injures many more? Do we deny the right to smoke even though its effects are known?

For youth to decide to call it quits is a tragedy. But is it any more tragic than the misuse of an auto, excessive drink or narcotic drugs? For the aged in pain, without means or friends, calling it quits is sensible. Shouldn't a civilized community permit the same choice to those for whom life has become a burden?

When P. W. Bridgman learned that he had an incurable ailment, he took his life. The note he left for his widow to share with others was unforgettable. In essence it revealed that he had decided to take his life while he was still able to do it. He feared that if his condition worsened he would not be able to see it through. He observed how cruel it is for society to inadvertently force a person to take his life before it is necessary. With sensible arrangements, he could have delayed his death until it was necessary.

As it does in our other attitudes, custom influences us in our views of suicide. Someday we may praise people who meet death on their own terms — at the time, place, and manner they decide upon.

"Not only is suicide a sin, but sin is suicide...sin...is, for instance, the ability to do as one pleases, to decide the purpose of life without rendering account to anyone else: 'you shall be like God'."

Suicide Is Sinful

Henri Blocher

A native of the Netherlands, Henri Blocher was educated at the Sorbonne, University of Paris, London Bible College and Gordon Divinity School. He has been on the faculty of French divinity schools and has authored several books including *The Three Friends* (1966) and *The Songs of the Servant* (1975). In the following viewpoint, Mr. Blocher argues that suicide is a sin and supports his argument with passages from the Bible.

Consider the following questions while reading:
1. **How does the author distinguish suicide from sacrifice?**
2. **In the author's opinion, what does the Bible say about suicide?**
3. **Why does the author equate suicide with sin? Do you agree?**

Taken from *Suicide* by Henri Blocher. ©1972 by Inter-Varsity Christian Fellowship of the USA and used by permission of InterVarsity Press.

Let us begin our consideration of the problem by defining *suicide*. In Lalande's *Vocabulary*, suicide is "the act of willfully causing one's own death in order to escape a condition of living that one esteems intolerable."

The word "willfully" eliminates certain automatic suicides, as in cases of mental illness or other cases where pathological determinism prevents us from speaking of "will"...

Some people have confused sacrifice and suicide. No doubt some acts called sacrifice are merely disguised suicides. Who will ever know the secret of certain heroic acts in battle or elsewhere? And, of course, there are borderline cases, for example, the soldier who prefers suicide to betraying his comrades because of torture. However, nothing can negate the radical difference between *giving one's life* and *taking it*. As a human act, sacrifice is diametrically opposed to suicide...

THE MORALITY OF SUICIDE

Surprisingly, the Bible does not give any precise statement on the morality of suicide...

The Scripture knows that the man who is tempted to commit suicide does not need another prohibition. His burden is already great enough, and Scripture does not overwhelm him. It does not make suicide, as did the Middle Ages, the crime of crimes, the shame of shames...

Although the Bible contains no precise statement about suicide, it does state commands and principles that relate to the problem. The commandmant "Thou shalt not kill" must apply since the suicide, in making himself the object of murder, still remains its subject. Above all, the suicide's fundamental desire to dispose of himself as he wills is incompatible with God's prerogatives in the Bible. The individual does not belong to himself; in a radical sense, he does not even belong to society. He belongs to God alone: "Behold, all souls are mine" (Ezek. 18:4).

God mercifully maintains the right of life and death — how great a burden it would be for man! "The Lord kills and brings to life" (I Sam. 2:6). God has given man the power of dying voluntarily only so that man may be capable of sacrifice — saying yes to God even if it means death. But God does not intend for that power to be abused by a man's saying yes to death when it is his own human will and not the will of God.

The fact that God reserves to himself the right of life and death explains why it is difficult to trace the frontier between suicide and sacrifice. The division is not made by some external law, it is made rather by the will of God, which is, at times, hidden to us...

THE PHENOMENON OF LIFE

Deep down I know that the phenomenon I call "life" is something utterly and totally beyond my doing; I did not create it, I am not sui generis of my own doing. Not having brought myself into the world, not having brought forth this briefly pulsating lifetime of mine, I do not own it, and in truth understand it but a little. I am merely a steward of a miracle, the witness of a wonder, to do with to the best of my ability.

This, in essence, is my quarrel with those who would promulgate suicide as the moral right and prerogative of the individual. Admittedly, life is often not easy, and sometimes circumstances are intolerable, defying our attempts at remedy. But that is a temporary problem with conditions and circumstances, not a flaw in the life process itself, and one does not shoot the messenger because one does not like the news he bears this time.

And it occurs to me that the proposition of the rightfulness of suicide confuses what is mine and thine.

Robert Treuer, *The Minneapolis Star*, April 22, 1981.

SIN BECOMES SUICIDE

Sin is the choosing of death. This theme recurs in Scripture from the first chapters of Genesis on. At times the idea of suicide, voluntary self-destruction, is clearly expressed. Divine wisdom declares (literally translated), "He who injures me attacks [mistreats] his own life; all those who hate me love death" (Prov. 8:36). The apostle Paul wrote concerning the flesh, that perverse tendency which corrupts our nature, "To set the mind on the flesh is death" (Rom. 8:6). This is the tragedy portrayed in Scripture: Man in his folly destroys himself.

We can easily find the typical traits of suicide in sin. Sin (in its Biblical sense) is, for instance, the will to do as one pleases, to decide the purpose of life without rendering account to anyone else: "You shall be like God" (Gen. 3:15). Suicide, for whatever reason, may be viewed as the ultimate realization of this project: Man has the right over his death as well as his life.

Yet the lie of this project is clear. Man is not God, he is not independent; he is not self–determinate, he must die. In order to maintain the fiction of his independence, he has but one course: He claims to *choose* death, to give death the yes which he refuses to God. This is why suicide is at the same time the convulsive claim to liberty and the ultimate flight when faced with the insupportable contradictions of life.

Further, one can discern in sin man's profound aggressiveness against himself, this obscure *destrudo* of which Deshaies speaks. It is necessary to take Paul's words literally (Rom. 8:6): The aim of the flesh is ultimately death. At the heart of sin, hidden but felt, there is a rage to defile and destroy, a mystery of iniquity.

We can now penetrate the origin of this mysterious destroyer. All that I am, I am by virtue of divine creation. All that I am bears the imprint of the Author. I must get rid of myself if I am to get rid of him. If sin is the frenzied will to independence and self–creation, it necessarily implies, then, the will to destroy that which I am. If I hate God, I must hate myself, for he has made me in his image. Kierkegaard called sin "the sickness unto death," the will's desperate attempt to be itself which leads to the will's desperate attempt to be no longer itself...

The suicide is more sensitive to the logic of sin than the average man. Most people live comfortably by constructing a shield of inconsistency behind which they can hold at bay their loneliness, their absurdity and their emptiness. For some, circumstances destroy this shield, and then they carry their commitment to its logical conclusions. So suicide is at the same time both sin and its mirror.

No, to invoke the rights of the collectivity or the dignity of man is not sufficient to dam up the *destrudo*. Neither is the

Henri Blocher

law of a remote and formidable God. Man needs to know the God of hope.

"In a civilized society suicide ought to be considered a quite proper way for a well-brought-up person to end his life."

Suicide Is Our Right

Mary Rose Barrington

Mary Rose Barrington, a lawyer, was educated at Oxford University and was admitted to the Bar in England in 1957. At the time she wrote the following viewpoint, Miss Barrington was a member of the Executive Committee of the Euthanasia Society in England. She holds that in a civilized society, suicide should be accepted as a proper way to end one's life if an individual so chooses.

Consider the following questions while reading:
1. What does Ms. Barrington mean when she claims that it is not suicide that should make one shudder, but the feeling of despair that causes many suicides?
2. Why are people who would like to end their lives reluctant to do so or even talk about it with their families, friends and doctors?
3. How does the author react to doctors who would not aid a patient in ending his life?

Mary Rose Barrington, "Apologia for Suicide," *Euthanasia and the Right to Death,* ed. A.B. Downing (Los Angeles: Nash Publishing, 1969). *Euthanasia and the Right to Death* edited by A.B. Downing, published by Peter Owen.

Indoctrination against suicide is regrettably to be found at all levels. In itself the tendentious expression 'to commit suicide' is calculated to poison the unsuspecting mind with its false semantic overtones, for, apart from the dangerous practice of committing oneself to an opinion, most other things commited are, as suicide once was, criminal offences. People are further influenced by the unhappy shadow cast over the image of suicide by the wide press coverage given to reports of suicide by students who are worried about their examinations, or girls who are upset over a love affair, or middle-aged people living alone in bed-sitting rooms who kill themselves out of depression — troubles that might all have been surmounted, given time. In pathetic cases such as these, it is not, as it seems to me, the act of suicide that is horrifying, but the extreme unhappiness that must be presumed to have induced it. Death from despair is the thing that ought to make us shudder, but the shudder is often extended to revulsion against the act of suicide that terminates the despair, an act that may be undertaken in very different circumstances...

People who insist that life must always be better than death often sound as if they are choosing eternal life in contrast to eternal death, when the fact is that they have no choice in the matter; it is death now, or death later. Once this fact is fully grasped it is possible for the question to arise as to whether death now would not be preferable...

THE NATURAL RIGHT TO DIE

Very little is 'natural' about our present-day existence, and least natural of all is the prolonged period of dying that is suffered by so many incurable patients solicitously kept alive to be killed by their disease. The sufferings of animals (other than man) are heart-rending enough, but a dying process spread over weeks, months or years seems to be one form of suffering that animals are normally spared. When severe illness strikes them they tend to stop eating, sleep and die. The whole weight of Western society forces attention on the natural right to live, but throws a blanket of silence over the natural right to die. If I seem to be suggesting that in a civilized society suicide ought to be considered a quite proper way for a well-brought-up person to end his life (unless he has the good luck to die suddenly and without warning), that is indeed the tenor of my argument; if it is received with astonishment and incredulity, the reader is referred to the reception of recommendations made earlier in the century that birth control should be practised and encouraged. The idea is no more extraordinary, and would be equally calculated to diminish the sum total of suffering among humankind...

CHOOSING DEATH

Attention is here being drawn to people who unfortunately have good reason to question whether or not they want to exercise their right to live; the minor infirmities of age, and relative weakness, and a slight degree of dependence on younger people who regard the giving of a helping hand as a natural part of the life-cycle, do not give rise to any such question. The question arises when life becomes a burden rather than a pleasure.

A LIVING DEATH

If it is a crime to kill a man, is it not a greater crime to sentence him to a living death? We did not wish to come into this world, so why should any man dictate to us how or when we decide to leave it?

Beverley Nichols, *Atlas*, May, 1975.

Many middle-aged people are heard to express the fervent wish that they will not live to be pain-ridden cripples, deaf, dim sighted or feeble-minded solitaries, such that they may become little else than a burden to themselves and to others. They say they hope they will die before any of these fates descend upon them, but they seldom affirm that they intend to die before that time; and when the time comes, it may barely cross their minds that they could, had they then the determination, take the matter into their own hands. The facile retort will often be that this merely goes to show that people do not really mean what they say and that like all normal, sensible folk, they really want to live on for as long as is physically possible. But this, I would suggest, is a false conclusion. They mean exactly what they say, but the conditions and conditioning of society make it impossible for them to act in accordance with their wishes. To face the dark reality that the future holds nothing further in the way of joy or meaningful experience, and to face the fact without making

119

some desperate and false reservation, to take the ultimate decision and act upon it knowing that it is a gesture that can never be repeated, such clear-sightedness and resolution demand a high degree of moral strength that cannot but be undermined by the knowledge that this final act of self-discipline would be the subject of head-shakings, moralizings and general tut-tutting.

How different it would be if a person could talk over the future with his family, friends and doctors, make arrangements, say farewells, take stock of his life, and know that his decision about when and how to end his life was a matter that could be the subject of constructive and sympathetic conference, and even that he could have his chosen ones around him at the last...

VOLUNTARY EUTHANASIA

That voluntary euthanasia is in fact assisted suicide is no doubt clear to most people, but curiously enough many who would support the moral right of an incurably sick person to commit suicide will oppose his having the right to seek assistance from doctors if he is to effect his wish...

Hostile sections of the medical profession will continue to assert that it is their business to cure and not to kill, and that in any case a patient who is in a miserable state from having his body invaded with cancers (or whatever) is in no state to make a decision about life and death. A patient who is in so pitiable a condition that he says he wishes to die is ipso facto not in a fit condition to make a reliable statement about his wishes. Arguments of this ilk seem at times to pass from black comedy to black farce. With the same sort of metaphysical reasoning it will be maintained that a patient who requested, and was given, euthanasia on Monday evening might, had he lived until Tuesday morning, have changed his mind. It has even been suggested that patients would, if voluntary euthanasia were available for incurable patients, feel themselves reluctantly obliged to ask for it to spare the nursing staff. And, as was remarked earlier, although laying down one's life in battle is generally considered praiseworthy, to lay down your life to spare yourself pointless suffering, to release medical staff so that they can tend people who would have some chance of living enjoyable lives given greater attention and assitance, to release your family and friends from anxiety and anguish, these motives are considered shocking. More accurately, a mere contemplation of these motives shocks the conditioned mind so severely

THIS DECLARATION is made

by _____

of _____

I DECLARE AS FOLLOWS:

If I should at any time suffer from a serious physical illness or impairment thought in my case to be incurable and expected to cause me severe distress or render me incapable of rational existence, then, unless I revoke this declaration or express a wish contrary to its terms, I REQUEST the administration of whatever quantity of drugs may be required to prevent my feeling pain or distress and, if my suffering cannot be otherwise relieved, to be kept continuously unconscious at a level where dreaming does not take place, AND
I DECLINE to receive any treatment or sustenance designed to prolong my life.
I ASK sympathetically disposed doctors to acknowledge the right of a patient to request certain kinds of treatment and to decline others, and I assure them that if in any situation they think it better for me to die than to survive, I am content to endorse their judgment in advance and in full confidence that they will be acting in my interests to spare me from suffering and ignominy, and also to save my family and friends from anguish I would not want them to endure on my behalf.

SIGNED _____

WE TESTIFY that the above named declarant signed this declaration in our presence, and appeared to appreciate its significance. We do not know of any pressure being brought upon him/her to make a declaration, and we believe it is made by his/her own wish. So far as we are aware, we do not stand to benefit by the death of the declarant.

Signed by _____

of _____

Signed by _____

of _____

that no rational comment can fight its way through to the surface; it is forced back by the death taboo...

There are many more doctors who are not at all opposed in principle to suicide, but who feel, whatever the logic of the matter, that they could not personally give a patient a lethal dose. This might be regarded as the same sort of squeamishness (for lack of a better word) that would prevent another sort of person from hitting a hopelessly injured bird over the head to put it out of its suffering. He would have to waste time filling a biscuit-tin with household gas, or taking the wounded creature to a clinic, or just looking for someone less squeamish. If really cowardly he may consider putting it back in the bushes in the delusive hope that it will make a recovery. But an honest person would have to admit that it was wrong in principle to let the animal suffer because of his 'sensitive' inaction...

THE GIFT OF DEATH

It is, of course, all too easy to make light of death when it seems far from imminent, and all too easy for someone who has had a satisfying life to say that other people, who may have had very little happiness, must learn to accept that their one and (ostensibly) only life must now cease. It may well turn out that we who insist on the right to come to terms with death before life becomes a burden may, when the time comes, be found to fail in our resolute purpose, and may end our lives by way of punishment in one of the appalling institutions provided by the state for the care of the aged. The failure may be due to physical helplessness coupled with the refusal of others to give the necessary help, or it may be due to a moral failure ascribable to personal weakness and the pressures of society, pressures that sometimes take a form too oblique to be recognized as twisters of the mind. Ending with a further complaint about linquistic misdirection, my final objection to tainted words is that a patient ending his own life, or a doctor assisting him to end it, is said to 'take life', just as a thief 'takes' property with the intention of depriving the owner of something he values. Whatever it is that is taken from a dying patient, it is nothing he wants to keep, and the act is one of giving rather than taking. The gift is death, a gift we shall all have to receive in due course, and if we can bring ourselves to choose our time for acceptance, so much the better for us, for our family, for our friends and for society.

"Suicide is always an act of absolute separation from the universe and other members of the human community."

Christianity Rejects Suicide

Ignace Lepp

Before his death, Ignace Lepp was a psychologist, psychotherapist and Catholic priest. His book, *Death and Its Mysteries* (1968), from which this viewpoint was taken, explores such topics as the experience of death, the death instinct, various aspects of suicide, the meaning of death and the immorality of the soul. Before his conversion to Catholocism, Father Lepp was a communist intellectual who taught philosophy at the University of Tiflis in Russia. What follows is the Christian and philosophical condemnation of suicide and a call to battle against the principal causes of suicide.

Consider the following questiions while reading:

1. **According to the author, what has been Christianity's position on suicide?**
2. **What is the author's position on suicide?**

Ignace Lepp, *Death and Its Mysteries* (New York: Macmillan Company, 1968). Reprinted with permission of Macmillan Publishing Co., Inc. from *Death and Its Mysteries* by Ignace Lepp. Copyright © 1968 by Macmillan Publishing Co., Inc.

I am speaking...as a psychologist rather than a moralist. But some readers may have the impression that I consider suicide a moral evil as well as a disease to be treated by medical science. The laws of many countries in fact condemn suicide as a crime.

Individualistic moralists and philosophers do not object in principle to a person's intention to commit suicide. Since everyone lives for himself and is the master of his own life, nothing is more logical than the right to renounce that life when the individual so pleases... Montaigne looked upon suicide as "the pleasure of affirming one's independence from nature by taking its place... The most voluntary death is the most beautiful. Our life depends on the will of others; death can depend on our own will." According to Henri de Montherlant, also a great admirer of the Stoics, suicide in addition procures the superior man "the pleasure of withdrawing from the lot of the common man," who docilely submits to the law of nature. And Dostoevski's Kirilov exclaimed, "Whoever wants supreme freedom must kill himself. He who dares to take his own life is God!"

CHRISTIANITY'S REJECTION OF SUICIDE

Perhaps Christianity's fundamental anti-individualism is nowhere more manifest than in its categorical rejection of a man's right to take his own life. Almost all moralists outside of Christianity are at least tolerant with respect to suicide and often admire it. The Christian believes that life is a gift of God over which man has no proprietary rights. He is a mere depository. Christian morality admits no distinction between murder and suicide. In both cases man is infringing upon God's rights. In practice, the Church is far more lenient toward murder, many forms of which she justifies, than toward suicide. Moreover, statistics show that suicide is more prevalent in Protestant countries than in Catholic ones. The reason for this is not only that Catholicism is especially categorical in its condemnation of suicide and refuses to grant it that "romantic" admiration it often enjoys elsewhere but, more importantly, that the Catholic doctrine of the mystical body reinforces the natural social bond among men and thus rejects the individualism more resolutely.

St. Thomas Aquinas based his rejection of suicide on the natural law, in much the same spirit as he tried to prove the perfect conformity of all Christian morality with the natural law. Like Aristotle, he begins with the principle that man does not belong to himself but to society, being by definition a "social animal." Suicide is a crime of homicide against society, depriving it of one of its members just as surely as if one had murdered his neighbor. On this point, Marxist morality is in perfect accord with Thomism. It does admit the legitimacy of suicide in the alienated world of capitalism, but absolutely nothing could justify it in the reconciled world of socialism. It is well known that the press in communist countries refuses to publish statistics on the number of suicides committed. A young Russian poet, taking advantage of the relative freedom that followed de-Stalinization, created something of a scandal by recalling that two of the most renowned poets of the revolution, Iessenine and Maiakovsky, committed suicide because they found the Communist regime intolerable. But St. Thomas does not argue that suicide is a crime in the name of social utilitarianism, but rather because it implies a violation of the duty of charity which every man has to himself as a creation of God.

ALL LIFE HAS MEANING

The courage to be, as expressed in Christian and Jewish thought, is more than the overcoming of the fear of death, although it includes that Stoic dimension. It is the courage to accept one's own life as having worth no matter what life may bring, including the threat of death, because that life remains meaningful and is regarded as worthy by God, regardless of what that life may be like.

Arthur J. Dyck, "An Alternative To the Ethic of Euthanasia," *To Live and To Die: When, Why, and How.*

MAN'S RIGHT TO COMMIT SUICIDE

It is important, however, to bear in mind that the problem of man's right to commit suicide has not always been construed in such simple terms, even by Christians. Thus Paul Landsberg, a German Catholic philosopher who was killed by the Nazis in 1944, confessed that he was psychologically and philosophically disposed to consider suicide justified in certain extreme circumstances... In his posthumous book, *The Moral Problem of Suicide*, Landsberg writes that the only argument against the right to commit suicide seems to him the duty every Christian has to imitate Christ. All arguments against suicide from natural law fail to stand up to critical examination and in any case are unconvincing in the eyes of a man who is sufficiently motivated psychologically to do away with a life that has grown intolerable. I agree with this position. Paul Landsberg in fact underwent a cruel death because of his conviction. He had been much impressed by St. Peter's admonition: "We must not, brethren, feel suffering for Christ, since he freely gave himself up to death for our salvation." At first, Landsberg was impressed by the last part of the sentence, which seemed to him to justify the kind of suicide that is motivated, not by boredom with life, but by the courage to die voluntarily. But later, after his own spritual outlook had matured, he saw in it an exhortation to imitate Christ. Since Christ had willingly submitted to violent death, Landsberg concluded that the Christian can imitate Christ by permitting himself to be killed by persecutors although not by killing himself.

Another philosopher of great spiritual insight, Louis Lavelle, found the idea of suicide repulsive. Since life is sacred, suicide is a "sacred crime." "The fact that one man refuses to live," he wrote, "seems to condemn all life." In my opinion, Lavelle is too severe in his judgment of suicide. It would be correct if men committed suicide in all liberty and lucidity. But we have seen that only the exceptional Stoics manage to take their lives with such a heightened awareness of what they are doing. In all other cases, the deep psychological motives for such a decision are the result of a serious inhibition of the life instinct or a crippling neurosis. Suicide represents a choice that is more or less determined.

AN ACT OF ABSOLUTE SEPARATION

If we could abstract from each suicide its subjective motives, I would be inclined to agree with Lavelle and Christian moralists in their categorical rejection of suicide. Whatever form it takes and under whatever conditions it happens, suicide is always an act of absolute separation from the universe and other members of the human community, a violent rupture of those relationships that are the very foundation of the human condition. He who commits suicide not only kills himself but in fact injures all life, since by his action he deprives it of his assistance. Thus, objectively, he rejects human and cosmic solidarity. Those who die naturally or accidentally also deprive the community of their help and are equally separated from it. But they have

126

no moral responsibility for their fate. This is the principal theoretical difference between natural death and suicide — and I consider accidental "natural" in this perspective. All death is sorrowful but suicide is tragic...

It seems, then, that we might offer a reasonably exact synthesis of contemporary theological, moral, sociological and psychological positions in the following manner: Suicide as such is reprehensible but we must have a great deal of understanding of and pity for the victims of suicide. The problem of suicide calls not so much for moral condemnation as for a battle against the principal causes of suicide, in particular against neurosis, loneliness and depression. The problem is, in fact, far more psychological than either sociological or moral.

"The decision we may make in choosing suicide is ours to make. It is our life we are giving up, our death we are arranging... We do not need to explain and excuse."

Common–Sense Suicide For The Elderly

Doris Portwood

Doris Portwood is a freelance writer. She is the author of several children's books as well as articles and stories for adults. Miss Portwood's most recent novel is set in India where she lived during World War II. In the following viewpoint, she argues that the aged should hold the legal right to arrange their own death by suicide.

Consider the following questions while reading:

1. For what kind of people does the author recommend common–sense suicide?
2. What does the author have to say about suicide prevention centers for younger people?
3. What does the author mean when she says "we give up our autonomy too easily when we become old and weak?" Do you agree?

Reprinted by permission of DODD, MEAD & COMPANY, INC. from *COMMON-SENSE SUICIDE: THE FINAL RIGHT* by Doris Portwood. Copyright © 1978 by Doris Portwood.

Almost no subject is barred from full discussion on TV talk shows or in the media.

Almost none.

An exception is rational suicide for the older person. It needs to be talked about and American women of social security age are the ones to start talking. There are so many of us — close to 15 million over-65 women and 145 for every 100 men in the same age group. And we live so long — outdistancing men by more than eight years.

IT WON'T HAPPEN TO ME

Senior American women have wealth and power. Yet hundreds of thousands end their lives in baffled misery in the near imprisonment of nursing home or hospital. Others are alone, clinging to a familiar place when it no longer provides the needed comforts. Still others, living with a relative, feel the disruption of their own lives and suffer guilt for the disruption they know their presence imposes.

Few would choose any of the common fates of the ailing elderly. How many of us, attending a friend or relative in her final days (or weeks, or months, or years) have said, "It won't happen to me. I'll take care of that."

But did we say it aloud?

It is time to say it loud and clear. And often. We can borrow a phrase from the new vocabulary and declare our intention to start a meaningful dialogue on common-sense suicide...

WE KNOW WHAT WE WANT

There is a continuing increase in suicide by the under-24 age group and few would argue against the need for suicide prevention centers, counselor hot-lines and research projects. When you are under 24, there is so much time to change your mind. People with many productive years to live should be helped to have that chance.

Equally, older persons should be accorded the courtesy of an assumption that we know what we want. By the time we reach 65 most of us have made many decisions. On a private decision we deserve the dignity of a respectful concurrence. When an older woman leaves a social gathering — perhaps an hour after dinner and when younger guests are settling

129

down to a game or a fresh drink — no one urges her to linger on. Someone may call a cab or offer a lift. She will receive thoughtful words during the process of departure, but no insistence on her staying. There is the assumption that she has, in fact, some good reason for going.

RIDICULOUS SUICIDE LAWS

Arguments for the right to voluntary euthanasia are essentially arguments for the right to suicide or, more precisely, the right to have others help one commit suicide if one is unable to carry it out oneself. Our ridiculous laws against suicide are based on the conviction that life is always better than death, and that anyone who decides differently for himself is certainly wrong and probably insane—a highly questionable presumption, at best.

Wayne Sage, *Human Behavior*, June, 1974.

When we have a good reason for voluntary departure from life, similar courtesy would be appreciated, but we cannot count on it. On the contrary, we can be quite sure it will *not* be forthcoming. Therefore we must demand it as a right of what has been called the U.S.A.'s fastest-growing minority: the aging...

SUICIDE THROUGH HISTORY

Down through recorded history, suicide has been many things to many people. To the early Greeks and Romans it was an honorable way to avoid capture by an enemy, to avoid the humiliation of defeat, and to evade death at an enemy's hands...

The early Christians brought a new attitude toward suicide by taking a fanatic delight in the prospect of instant salvation. There was no shortage of candidates for the tortures of the arena: a martyr's death meant a reserved seat among the blessed in heaven. These suicides were, in today's language, passive rather than active. The primitive Christians did not fall on the sword or hold the hemlock cup to their own lips, but they walked willingly — men, women and children — into situations (often deliberately provoked situations) that meant not only death but death of a most grim variety...

RELIGIOUS BELIEFS

No matter how or when the legalization of old-age suicide may come about, many who are tempted will continue to be deterred by religious beliefs. The awesomeness of the idea of "God-given life" persists almost as stubbornly as our durable old bodies. The sanctity of life, regardless of the condition of that "life," is being defended on various fronts and will continue to be defended. But opposition to orthodox sanctity-of-life views also is strong, both within and without the various religious communities. The changing status of divorce, contraception and abortion (at a time when a religious revival also is noted) shows a trend toward new church-vocabulary definitions in relation to many moral and ethical questions of today's society...

AUTONOMY REPLACES AUTHORITY

Our era is, according to the popular press, a time of accent on *Me.* Bugged perhaps by being too frequently a mere computer number, today's individual shouts her or his identity and rights.

Even the old — our fastest-growing minority — have the right to say *Me too.* We have no obligation to abandon our preferences and opinions just because our weakening voices may be outshouted.

The decision we may make in choosing suicide is *ours* to make. It is our life we are giving up, our death we are arranging. The choice does not infringe on the rights of others. We do not need to explain and excuse.

Daniel C. Maguire, a theology professor whose *Death by Choice* examines in some depth the moral aspects of euthanasia, accents that "Many people have difficulty believing that they have moral authority over their dying. One of the principal reasons why this question is opening up for reconsideration today is that the idea of authority is being rethought."

The rethinking contributes to the "me" attitude. It gives us autonomy if we have the courage to take it and use it. Psychiatry professor Thomas Szasz, in his *Ceremonial*

Chemistry, says on the subject: "Autonomy is the death knell of authority, and authority knows it: hence the ceaseless warfare of authority against the exercise, both real and symbolic, of autonomy — that is, against suicide, against masturbation, against self-medication, against the proper use of language itself!"

AGE DIFFERENCE AND SUICIDE

There is an unarguable difference between planned suicides among the elderly and the impulsive acts of young people who may be supersensitive, temporarily depressed, or simply lacking the maturity to be objective about the reality of their lives.

Doris Portwood, *Common-Sense Suicide.*

We give up our autonomy too easily when we become old and weak. Many who wish to die will live on because of their family's pride, their doctor's principles, their formal affiliation with a church, or a community attitude that sees suicide as a blot on the record. The choice will be made by "them." The suffering will be for "me."

It need not be so.

"A suicidal youth...may not wait for life to teach him that his feelings are normal and understandable, or that there are ways of dealing with them."

The Need To Educate Adolescents About Suicide

Charlotte P. Ross

Charlotte P. Ross is executive director of the Suicide Prevention and Crisis Center of San Mateo County, California. The co-author of *Suicide in Youth and What You Can Do About It – A Guide for Students,* she has been instrumental in developing pilot programs for training school personnel and students in suicide prevention. Miss Ross is also the author of *Standards for Suicide Prevention and Crisis Intervention Centers* (1974) and the editor of *Newslink.* In the following viewpoint, she explains what motivates students to attempt suicide and claims that since potential suicides most frequently contact their friends, it is essential that all adolescents be educated as potential rescuers.

Consider the following questions while reading:
1. **Explain the example Ms. Ross gives as "a dangerous myth" about suicide. Why does she say the myth is dangerous?**
2. **Why does the author feel it is essential that all adolescents be educated about suicide?**

From "Teaching Children the Facts of Life and Death: Suicide Prevention in the Schools," a chapter by Charlotte P. Ross for a book in progress by Norman L. Farberow.

The facts of death are as essential to the education of the young — and as intently sought — as the facts of life. In both instances adolescents want to know because these subjects touch their deepest and most private feelings, because their present and future actions will be affected by their knowledge or lack of knowledge, and because societal taboos have made the information difficult to obtain.

In too many instances, however, there is an additional motivation to learn about suicide. What the increasing rate of youth suicides means to many adolescents is that they knew, or know of, someone their own age who died by his own hand.

ATTRACTED AND REPELLED BY SUICIDE

For a growing number of adolescents there is an even more compelling motivation. These are the youngsters who have been deeply hurt in their short lives. They are suffering and it seems to them that the pain will never end. They want desperately to know about suicide, because they are terribly attracted and terribly repelled by the idea of it.

When youngsters who want to learn are not provided reliable information, they seek out what they can as best they can. Often, their sources are rumor and speculation, and their experts are other teenagers. With a subject as fraught with dangerous myths, half-truths and misconceptions as suicide, the results can be tragic. For example, the belief that suicidal impulses indicate self-pity, inadequacy, or "insanity" may further damage a youth's already fragile self-esteem, and add a secondary panic reaction to an existing depression.

The ability to understand and cope with depression appears to be a learned faculty and, in most instances, experience is the teacher. A suicidal youth, however, may not wait for life to teach him that his feelings are normal and understandable, or that there are ways of dealing with them. It is our contention that if he is to learn this in time, a part of his education must be directed toward that goal...

Suicide intrudes upon the lives of not some, but most, teenagers. It is the third leading cause of death among adolescents in the United States, exceeded only by accidents and homicides. Every year, it is estimated, about 400,000 young people between the ages of 15 and 24 attempt suicide...

THE DARK SIDE OF ADOLESCENCE

It would seem that adolescence, which has been described as "synonymous with energy, enrichment, joy, promised satisfactions, invincible hopes — that is, with everything one associates with life" has its dark side. The statistics indicate that for more than half our adolescents, hope is not invincible and the promise is not always kept.

THE CRUELEST MONTH

Those who are familiar with the clues, the warning signals of an adolescent contemplating suicide, may well be able to save a young life. Knowing something about the time of greatest danger, for instance, can help. The poet T.S. Eliot wrote, "April is the cruelest month..."— and suicide rates bear that out. Spring, April particularly, is the time of year when most suicides, and episodes of depression as well, occur.

Arthur S. Freese, *Adolescent Suicide: Mental Health Challenge*, Public Affairs Pamphlet #569.

Adolescence is also a period of transition between childhood and adulthood. To become an adult, the child must "put away childish things." He must give up his dependence and become an autonomously functioning individual; he must understand and establish his sexual being; he must search for his identity, and also for the path that will allow him to express that identity through relationships and career. These are the historical tasks of adolescence, but today's teenagers must accomplish this while their world is shaken by social tremors that seriously strain their traditional support systems. The families of these teenagers are likely to be extended, not by grandparents or aunts and uncles, but by divorce and remarriage. Those who traditionally offered him support, guidance, and experience are likely — in these "reconstituted" families — to be distracted from his needs by the dilemmas arising from their own changing roles and relationships.

The path to adulthood is a rocky one to climb unaided. It can be frustrating, disappointing — and depressing. Indeed, for adolescents, depression seems to go with the territory. In a study of 5,600 high school youngsters, depression was shown to be second only to colds, sore throats and coughs in frequency.

It is perhaps the very commonness of teenage depression that clouds its inherent danger. Maggie Scarf, noting that depression has been referred to as the common cold of psychiatric disorders, adds, "But it is also the only one with a significant mortality rate. It has been said that 95 percent of people come out of depression unless suicide intervenes. That's one hell of an intervention."

Clearly, the danger is present, it is extensive, and it is lethal. Adolescence is, in reality, one of the more perilous parts of life's journey, and there is a critical need to prepare youngsters traversing it to survive its major hazards.

THE NEED TO EDUCATE RESCUERS

In addition to the need for adolescents to gain an understanding and a means of coping with their depressive or suicidal feelings, there is another compelling need for providing them with such an education. The persons most frequently contacted by adolescents contemplating or planning suicide, and who therefore would be their most likely rescuers, are their friends. As potential rescuers, they need to be able to effectively respond to their suicidal friends...

It appeared (in a recent survey) that the teenager's choice of confidants was influenced to some degree by the struggle with dependency conflicts that are an integral part of this stage of development. Often, adults were apprehensively viewed — from the far side of the generation gap — as being unable to understand, but quite able to interfere. Peers, however, allied in a common bond of shared needs, were viewed as offering the greater possibility of empathy, the greater assurance of non-interference and, of extreme importance, greater respect for maintaining a confidence.

However, some of the very qualities that make peers the confidants of choice also make them dangerously inadequate as counselors and rescuers. Adolescents' sacred commitment to keeping a confidence, their disinclination — or inability — to actively intervene, and their lack of knowledge regarding what could or should be done, makes the awesome responsibility that may be imposed upon them an uncertain undertaking at best...

Yet, while adolescents may be woefully unprepared for the rescuer role, they are likely to fall heir to it nonetheless. It would seem that since adolescents determine whom their helpers are to be (and although we can strive to increase the choices acceptable to them, their peers are, and likely will continue to be, a major resource) every effort should be extended to equip them to deal more effectively with such critical encounters...

DEAR ANN LANDERS

Dear Ann: *Why can't a person leave this world when he is ready by simply taking a pill and going to sleep forever? I am sure many people would welcome such a blessed release. Why haven't doctors thought of this? When animals suffer, it is considered merciful to put them to sleep. I believe every doctor should be permitted to give his patients the same considerations animals get. Don't you?* **A Reader in St. Louis.**

Ann says: *Thousands of people do exactly what you have suggested every year. It's called suicide. The flaw in your reasoning is this: Many pills can be obtained by prescription only because people must be protected against killing themselves while in a depressed state or at a time when they are suffering temporary physical pain or emotional distress.*

Many people who are enjoying life today will tell you there have been times when they would have taken a handful of pills if they had had them—and it's a good thing they didn't. Death is permanent.

Ann Landers, *Minneapolis Tribune*, February 13, 1979. Reprinted by permission of Ann Landers and Field Newspaper Syndicate.

We believe that the prevalence of teenage depression, the suicidal impulses that often accompany it, and the teenager's preference for peer confidants indicate a need for prevention programs which educate adolescents both as potential victims and potential rescuers.

ABILITY TO EMPATHIZE

SUICIDE -- YOU DECIDE

The ability to empathize, to see a problem from another person's vantage point, is a skill that must be widely developed if human problems like euthanasia, abortion and suicide are to be resolved.

Three very different suicide situations are described below.

Instructions

STEP 1. The class should break into groups of four to six students.

STEP 2. Each student should carefully read the three suicide situations.

STEP 3. Each group should next discuss the following questions, and attempt to reach a consensus.

1. What is the motivation for suicide in each case?
2. Which suicide is least justifiable? Which is most justifiable? Is suicide ever justifiable?

STEP 4. Each group member, if they feel comfortable doing so, should express how they think they would react if they were the subject in each of the three suicides described.

STEP 5. If they wish, group members may tell of suicides with which they are familiar. They should describe the circumstances involved and what they believe the subject's motivation was. They should also describe their reaction to the suicide.

STEP 6. The entire class should discuss and compare the small groups' conclusions.

Suicide ONE

SPOKANE, Wash. (AP) — A 38-year-old man committed suicide because he wanted his sister to have one of his kidneys but he died in vain because the organ was unusable by the time his body was found, medical authorities and the man's family said Thursday.

Melvin S. Gordon, whose sister suffers from kidney disease, shot himself in the head Wednesday night, investigators said. A note pinned to his shirt said: "Get my kidney within one hour"...

Gordon's body was found in his car in the driveway at the emergency room entrance of Sacred Heart Medical Center, according to hospital spokesman Mike Heinrich. A discharged patient found Gordon slumped over the steering wheel of the car several minutes after he died.

But kidneys must be removed from a person's body at the moment of death and kept functioning with blood circulation equipment to avoid tissue deterioration, Heinrich said. Gordon's kidneys were atrophied by the time his death was reported, he said.

However, Gordon was carrying a donor's card and his corneas were taken for use by an eye bank.

Gordon had been depressed recently, partly because of a pending seasonal furlough from his job as a boilermaker and a one-month leave of absence he had taken, his wife said Thursday. But she said his greatest concern had been his sister's poor health and he had said several times he would give almost anything to help her.

Taken from *Los Angeles Times* of March 10, 1978.

Suicide TWO

WOMAN BURNS HERSELF TO DEATH IN U.N. PROTEST

A young woman clad in a white gown burned herself to death Monday evening in front of the U.N. Palace in Geneva, Switzerland. United Press International said it received a phone call saying there would be a spectacular demonstration because the United Nations was "not doing its job." Two photographers arrived at the scene about the same time. They saw the woman on the lawn and thought she was the

United Press International

first to arrive for the demonstration. As they walked toward her, she burst into flames. A bus driver who was parked nearby rushed to her with a fire extinguisher, but was too late to save her. Geneva police did not release the woman's name or nationality, but said she was 24 years old. Papers and posters presumably left in the area by the woman said: "The United Nations holds the lives and hopes of billions in its decisions, but the delegates prefer a luxurious life to their human responsibilities." "A flaming torch in the dark night of exploitation."

United Press International, October 3, 1978.

Suicide THREE

One of the best known "pact" cases was the attempted double suicide of Dr. Henry Pitney Van Dusen and his wife in

140

1975. Dr. Van Dusen had been president of the Union Theological Seminary and enjoyed world recognition. He and his wife had long supported the concept of voluntary euthanasia and Dr. Van Dusen had gone on record as early as 1946, along with forty other religious leaders, to register that support. Dr. Van Dusen suffered a stroke in 1970 and lost the speaking facility that had been such a large part of his life. His wife was arthritic. Both were becoming more and more dependent on others.

They came to their decision in late January 1975 and both took large doses of sleeping pills. As in many pacts, one succumbed peacefully (Mrs. Van Dusen) but the other did not. Dr. Van Dusen was hospitalized and lived until mid-February. The actual circumstances of the deaths were not made public until after Dr. Van Dusen's passing. Then the couple's simple note was released, and public opinion — both pro and con — had its day. One of the pros suggested that, "Far from being the ultimate failure of liberal Protestantism, it (suicide) is the ultimate triumph." And one of the cons stated that "Our profound sin is to believe that we are 'in charge' and determine our fate and the fate of the world."

The Van Dusens' own note commented that "Nowadays it is difficult to die," and added, "We feel that this way we are taking will become more usual and acceptable as the years pass."

Taken from *Common Sense Suicide* by Doris Portwood, pp. 69-70.

BIBLIOGRAPHY

The following list of periodical articles deals with the subject matter of this chapter.

J. Chase-Marshall — *Teenage Suicide,* **Good Housekeeping**, May, 1979, p. 96.

Christianity Today — *End of Life*, May 6, 1977, p. 57.

W. Coleman — *The Death They Whisper About,* **Christianity Today**, September 23, 1977, p. 38.

Annette Drabinsky — *Winning the Suicide Sweepstakes,* **Human Behavior**, January, 1979, p. 14.

C.G. Felsenthal — *Teen Suicide,* **Seventeen**, April, 1979, p. 184.

S. Gardner — *Suicidal Behavior,* **Senior Scholastic**, January 9, 1981, p. 9.

H. Hendin — *A Saner Policy on Suicide,* **Psychology Today**, May, 1979, p. 115.

Beverly Howze — *Black Suicides,* **Human Behavior**, February, 1979, p. 59.

Human Behavior — *Death on Demand*, February, 1976, p. 54.

Karen Kenyon — *A Survivor's Notes,* **Newsweek**, April 30, 1979, p. 17.

Charles Krauthammer — *PBS's Invitation to Suicide: Death of a Princess,* **The New Republic**, July 5-12, 1980, p. 14.

J. Marks — *Suicide: The Myths and Facts,* **Teen**, May, 1979, p. 14.

M.P. Scott and E. Kiester, Jr. — *Suicide: Let's Separate Fact From Fiction,* **Better Homes and Gardens**, April, 1977, p. 66.

D.K. Shah and M. Gosnell — *Rational Suicide? Case of J. Roman,* **Newsweek**, July 2, 1979, p. 87.

J. Stein — *Coming Home (High Suicide Rate Among Vietnam Veterans),* **The Progressive**, April, 1981, p. 10.

Time — *M.D. Suicides,* February 16, 1981, p. 57.

Time — *Suicide Belt,* September 1, 1980, p. 56.

Chapter 4

PROBLEMS OF
DEATH

Do
Funeral Homes
Exploit Us?

"Many members of this $6.4 billion industry take advantage of the family's grief and ignorance"

The Funeral Industry Lives Off the Dead

Thomas J. Reese

Thomas J. Reese, a Jesuit priest, earned a doctorate in political science from the University of California, Berkeley. A former legislative director for Taxation with Representation, a public interest tax reform lobby, he is the author of *The Politics of Taxation*. Presently, Father Reese is an associate editor of *America* magazine. In the following viewpoint, he argues that many in the funeral industry take unfair advantage of families during their time of grief and clarifies some misconceptions about what is legally required for funerals.

Consider the following questions while reading:
1. **Why does Mr. Reese claim the deceased's family is not in a position to make intelligent decisions regarding funerals?**
2. **What are some of the common methods Mr. Reese accuses the funeral industry of using to take advantage of the bereaved family?**
3. **Why does Mr. Reese accuse churches of having a conflict of interest with the funeral industry?**

Thomas J. Reese, "The Funeral Industry: Living Off the Dead," *America,* June 23, 1979. Reprinted with permission of American Press, Inc., 106 West 56th Street, New York, NY 10019, © 1979. All rights reserved.

At some point in your life, you will probably have to deal with a funeral parlor to prepare for burial a friend or relative. Someday, someone will have to do the same for you. With the average cost of a funeral over $2,000, for many families this will be the third most costly purchase — after buying a home and a car — you or your loved ones will make. But the arrangements are usually made with much less thoughtful consideration than the costs warrant. The deceased's family are not in a position to make very intelligent decisions because of grief, time pressures for arranging the funeral and general lack of knowledge about death–related legal and religious requirements.

TAKING ADVANTAGE OF GRIEF

Most families depend on the funeral director's advice and counsel for the funeral. But the Federal Trade Commission (F.T.C.) has found that many members of this $6.4 billion industry take advantage of the family's grief and ignorance and, like maggots, live off the dead.

Many funeral directors, for example, refuse to give specific price information over the telephone or in the funeral home until after a purchase has been made. Some directors fail to inform families accurately about the legal requirements for funeral merchandise such as coffins or for services such as embalming.

These directors are, of course, a disgrace to the industry and perhaps a small minority, but the industry itself has done little to discourage them. In fact, it has actively opposed attempts by the F.T.C. to stop these abuses through regulations.

The industry argues that the abuses are not widespread and that consumers are in fact well treated by funeral homes. A survey sponsored by the National Funeral Directors' Association found that 88 percent of the respondents were very satisfied with the funeral director's service, and 90 percent thought the funeral director adequately explained the choices the consumer could make. The F.T.C. felt, however, that consumer satisfaction was not a good indicator of abuses because purchasers frequently do not know what is being done to them...

WHAT YOU SHOULD KNOW

While laws governing the care of the dead vary from state to state, in general here are some things you should know about them before you see a funeral director.

Prior to the Civil War, embalming was not commonly practiced in this country. Embalming began at that time in order to preserve the bodies of deceased soldiers so that they could be shipped home. In earlier times, it was common for members of the family to wash and prepare the body for burial. Frequently a member of the family or the local carpenter would make the coffin.

Today, according to the F.T.C., "no state has an absolute legal requirement that remains must be embalmed in all circumstances... The special circumstances under which embalming may be required include death by communicable disease, interstate transportation, holding the body beyond a specific length of time and, in Kansas, burial in a mausoleum and intercounty transportation of the remains."

THE VALUE OF DEATH

The value of a living body, even in this inflationary period, is still only about 75 cents. But when that body is dead, it becomes profitable—to everyone involved in the funeral business. A living person might not be worth a nickel to anybody, but that body can cost plenty of hard earned insurance or savings before it gets a final resting place.

Virginia K. Stanton, Letters to the Editor, *Milwaukee Journal*, January 21, 1979.

Embalming has been defended by some in the funeral industry as a public health measure. But the F.T.C. reported: "A review of the evidence suggests that the empirical basis for the public health necessity claimed for embalming is at best dubious." Dr. Bruce Dull, assistant director for programs at the Public Health Service's Center for Disease Control, said: "We have yet to see any data indicating that there is a public health problem in the United States today associated with unembalmed or ineffectively embalmed cadavers"...

EMBALMING: RELIGIOUS VIEW

There is, of course, no religious requirement for embalming. In fact, it is forbidden by Orthodox Jews, who consider it a desecration of the dead. Thus, the women who came to Jesus' tomb on Easter morning came to anoint His body with spices but not to embalm it.

Some funeral directors have falsely claimed that embalming would protect the deceased from decay forever. But the purpose of embalming is really only to preserve the body for a short period of time. No matter how well embalmed, the body will eventually decay. At best, it will end up looking like King Tut — not a pretty sight once the gold and jewels are removed...

The casket is usually the most expensive item purchased for the funeral. Since funeral homes make a commission from the sale of caskets, they give careful consideration to how the caskets are presented to their customers. The F.T.C. found that many funeral homes display their cheapest casket in a soiled condition or in an unattractive color.

Worse yet, many do not even put their cheapest coffin in the showroom... A survey of 116 funeral homes in Maine found that one-third failed to display their least expensive casket...

MISCONCEPTIONS ABOUT CREMATION

Many Catholics are still under the false impression that their dead must be buried and not cremated. This is no longer true, although the church's "preference" is "for the custom of burying the dead in a grave or tomb..." But as is explained in the introduction to the *Rite of Funerals:* "Christian funeral rites are permitted for those who choose to have their bodies cremated unless it is shown that they have acted for reasons contrary to Christian principle." Thus, unless the reason for choosing cremation is a disbelief in the Resurrection or some other Christian principle, cremation is permitted...

Numerous people, myself included, have been told that a casket is required even if the body is going to be cremated. However, no state has an explicit casket requirement...

After a five-year study of the funeral industry, the F.T.C. staff drafted a series of regulations in 1978 to protect consumers from unfair and anticompetitive practices by funeral home operators. These regulations were then subject to public comment and were weakened because of complaints from the funeral industry...

That some members of the funeral industry have been able to treat the public unfairly, while working with churches to bury the dead, is a disgrace. Most pastors will not give their parishioners advice about funeral services. some do not want to appear to favor one funeral director over another. Most do not know the field themselves and, therefore, would not want to give advice on something in which they have no expertise. Others, perhaps, are influenced by the lucrative donations or advertising in the parish bulletin that come from funeral homes.

Dioceses are no better. Funeral homes advertise in the diocesan paper, which may be reluctant, as a result, to run an expose of the local funeral industry. Since churches or dioceses frequently own cemeteries, they have a conflict of interests because of their relationships with the industry. An average sized cemetery can easily net a quarter of a million dollars a year. It is not surprising, then, that although churches take positions on everything from the Panama Canal Treaty to SALT II, most have avoided the issue of regulating the funeral industry...

PLANNING YOUR OWN FUNERAL

If after reading this article you decide to prepare your own

'... And what the heck is this item here, "rental of burial tux for deceased, five hundred dollars per year"?'

funeral, there are a number of things you should keep in mind. It is best to leave written instructions for your funeral, since that will avoid arguments among the family over what you wanted. Make sure someone knows where you have left these instructions.

The instructions should specify whether you want to be cremated or not, whether you want a casket or not, whether you want to be embalmed, how much should be spent on flowers and where your remains should be placed. Some people also wish at this time to donate their bodies or some organs of it to a hospital or medical school. If a body is accepted by a medical school, the cost for burial or cremation is, of course, eliminated. Since many medical schools have received in this way more bodies than they need, alternative plans should be made in case your body is rejected.

These decisions can have a tremendous financial effect on the family you leave behind. As the F.T.C. noted: "Funeral costs vary enormously among different funeral homes and among different kinds of dispositions and ceremonies. For example, the cost of donating a body to medical science may be only a minimal fee for transportation of the body; an immediate cremation may cost $250-$350; an immediate ground burial may cost $420-$500; a cremation after a funeral service may cost $650-$800; and a typical traditional funeral with ground burial may cost $2,200-$2,400 for both funeral and burial expenses." The sky is the limit, of course, for extras.

It is your body. Plan now, die later.

"Funerals are for the living...they cause us to come together in a way we otherwise never do"

Funeral Homes Help Diminish Grief

Howard C. Raether & Robert C. Slater

Howard C. Raether has been associated with the National Funeral Directors since 1948 and became executive director in 1971. A graduate of Marquette University, Raether is the author and editor of numerous books in the funeral industry field. Robert C. Slater is Professor and Director of the Mortuary Science Department at the University of Minnesota. In the following viewpoint, the authors offer answers to certain relevant questions about funeral services, funeral directors and funerals in general.

Consider the following questions while reading:
1. **Why is the funeral a valuable experience?**
2. **What is the purpose of viewing a dead body?**
3. **What is the cost of the average American funeral?**
4. **What is the role of the funeral director?**

This reading was excerpted from a statement sent to the editor by the authors.

"Insofar as our funerals meet...needs as they are present in the individual mourners, the funeral is an experience of value."

Rev. Paul E. Irion, Professor of Pastoral Care at the Lancaster Theological Seminary of the United Church of Christ, made this statement in 1956 when death truly was a taboo subject. Now that it is one of the most discussed topics of the day, it is meaningful to examine the immediate post-death customs of our culture to determine if they are only a vestige or whether they have value for those who mourn.

The Funeral Is Not of American Origin

The American funeral director did not invent the funeral. Since the beginning of recorded history, the customs of most cultures include viewing the dead body and then burying or cremating it with ceremony. In doing this, psychologists say, people confirm the reality of what has happened. The confrontation of the dead body makes it easier to realize that the dead person is no longer alive. Most bereaved persons need social support during the major separation crisis that follows death. The sorrows of the survivors also may become the sorrows of those who attend the rite or ceremony. In the appropriate setting, if the bereaved is religiously oriented, his or her faith can be affirmed by the rites, symbols and ceremonies which become a part of the funeral service. In this sense, the funeral can provide the bereaved with a proper vehicle for mourning because just as joy shared is joy increased, grief shared is grief diminished...

Questions and Answers About the American Funeral

Dr. Robert Fulton, Director of the Center for Death Education and Research at the University of Minnesota, explains that we in the United States today have the first death-free generation in the world. Millions of Americans have never seen a dead body except during a movie or a television show, on a highway or battle field. Few have had "funeral experience"...

In such a setting, it is not surprising that young and old alike have many questions about death. Here are some of the most often-asked questions and answers relating to funerals and funeral service.

What is a funeral?

West Coast psychiatrist Dr. William M. Lamers, Jr., says

that the funeral is "an organized, purposeful, flexible, time limited, group centered response to death"...

World renowned composer-conductor Leonard Bernstein wrote an article adopted from a eulogy he gave at the funeral for singer, Jennie Tourel. The first and second paragraphs of the piece, which was in the December 9, 1973, *New York Times,* said in part:

It took me a long time to discover the values of a funeral ceremony. I had always abhorred and avoided them as pomposities — pompes funebres — and as a poor way to say goodbye, a needlessly public way of paying one's private last respects. And then, on one especially personal occasion, I suddenly discovered what everyone else had apparently known all along; that funerals are for the living, that they cause us to come together in a way we otherwise never do, to lean on one another, to feel the communality of emotions, to cry together, and — yes — to rejoice together, to rejoice in the one who has caused this coming together...

Should the body be present during the funeral?

Yes. Author and lecturer Dr. Edgar N. Jackson says:

At its best a funeral should help people face reality, express feelings and gain group support. The late Erich Lindemann, who was Professor of Psychiatry at Harvard, said that nothing helps people face reality like the moments of truth when the living confront the dead. This has in most cultures and in most times been central in the funeral process. To avoid confronting death is to pervert the purpose of the funeral and reduce its efficiency. The change of status death brings can best be faced through recognizing physical death as the basic step toward honest and healthful mourning.

What is the purpose of viewing a dead body?

Psychiatrists claim that the old adage, "seeing is believing," is useful for many bereaved people. Viewing the dead may be of greater importance today than ever before for three reasons. First, an increasing proportion of people die away from home, often in distant medical institutions, and the bereaved may not grasp death's reality without seeing the body. Second, there is an increasing proportion of deaths which follow a lingering illness, and the bereaved may have unpleasant memories of the wasted and emaciated appearance of the dying person. Third, there is an increasing proportion of people who die under tragic circumstances, and the bereaved may be unwilling to accept such a death following a tragedy. Viewing the dead body helps make those who survive more aware of the reality of death.

FUNERAL IS FOR THE LIVING

"The funeral is not for the dead person. The value is for the living. Many studies show that we really need the struggling and decisions involved in planning a funeral. By making decisions, we pull ourselves out of the cocoon of withdrawal."

Dick Obershaw, *Minneapolis Tribune*, May 1, 1975.

During a lingering illness, a person's face may be disfigured with the effects of pain or malignancy. As a result of an accident or a violent death, an entire body may be disfigured. In both instances, proper preparation and, when necessary, restoration help to modify and remove the ravages of disease or the marks of violence. Preparation, restoration, and the use of cosmetics are not meant to make the dead look alive; they are intended to help provide an acceptable image for recalling the deceased.

Viewing has been found to be therapeutic for people of all ages. It may be especially helpful for a child who has experienced the death of a relative or close friend. Instead of fantasizing with a vivid imagination, with the dead body present, the child may be able to comprehend the real meaning of death.

Is it an ordeal for survivors of a death to receive people during visitation, calling hours, the wake or shivah?

No. Generally, the funeral is a ceremony to which no one is invited but all may attend. The same is true of the condolence or sympathy visit; not only is a visit appreciated, but it also is often most helpful to the bereaved.

What the visitor must overcome is the mistaken belief that the mourner prefers to be alone. Moreover, pain suffered in solitude is heavier to bear than pain which is shared. By just being there, the relative, friend or neighbor testifies to the reality of the death as well as to the support of the living community.

Whatever the participation, there is the important opportunity to express feelings and offer sympathy to the bereaved. Some persons may want to avoid this kind of interaction because they do not know what to say or how to say it. This is not a valid concern. Many times the very presence of a person speaks to the fact that life must go on, especially if that person has experienced the death of someone close...

Are there any important general considerations one must have in mind when considering what is to be paid for a funeral and final disposition of a body?

Yes! The funeral is usually selected by the family of the deceased. Their wants, desires and needs must be considered. Generally, their decision is rooted in religious and ethnic customs, family preferences and traditions and the customs and traditions of their community. Then, too, the economy of an area has its effect on funeral costs, just as it does on the cost of other services and commodities.

As in most "purchases," the price paid for something

relates to the need for and the value in the service and/or the merchandise. In this regard, in Dr. Colin Murray Parkes' book, *Bereavement*, he writes: "What is the cash value of a funeral? This is a question easier to ask than to answer."

The value of a funeral as to its dollar cost should be seen in three perspectives. Its cost should be commensurate with the family's ability to pay for it. Its lasting value should be seen as an investment that makes the family feel good not only on the day of its selection but long after the funeral is over. Lastly, it must have utilitarian value in order that the family can experience that value (both psychological and economical) received for dollars spent.

NO GOOD SUBSTITUTE FOR FUNERALS

I've seen case after case of depression caused by the inability of patients—young and old—to work through their feelings after a death. I've found that people are often better off if they have a funeral to focus their feelings on. That lets them do the emotional work necessary in response to the loss...

I see constant evidence that the problems resulting from a serious separation—through death, divorce, or other means—can have great psychological impact. If these problems remain unresolved, grave emotional trouble can result later...

Are there any satisfactory funeral substitutes—a memorial service, for example? In my opinion, there aren't.

William M. Lamers, Jr. (Psychiatrist, Kentfield, California) in "Funerals are Good For People—M.D.'s Included," *Medical Economics*, June 23, 1969.

Are funerals appropriate for stillborns, infants who survive only for a matter of days and small children?

Yes. To the parents, the stillborn or child who is only a few days old has already been very much a part of their lives for as

155

long as nine plus months. They will experience all of the emotions of grief, which many times will be in even sharper focus and greater intensity. The funeral permits them to face the reality of the death, choose appropriate means of expression of their grief and, most importantly, experience the support of those who are close to them. Age is no determinate factor in the experience of grief. The process of bereavement and mourning is as important for the resolution of that grief whether the deceased is one day or one hundred years old.

What statistics are available as to what a funeral costs?

Funeral costs are primarily determined by those arranging for the service.

The 1980 study of the National Funeral Directors Association to ascertain 1979 funeral service income and expense patterns involved 138,551 deaths. Its findings plus inflationary factors indicate that the greatest number of funeral selections in 1980 will be in the $1,500 to $2,500 range. There will, of course, be offerings and selections below and above this range.

In 1979, the average "total adult" funeral selected was $1,653. This average did not include children's funerals, welfare adult and partial adult services which usually are offered at a lower price than total adult services. With these other than total adult services included, the average expenditure was $1,422.

(The statistics in the two paragraphs above are for professional services, facilities, transportation and the casket supplied by the funeral establishment. They do not include the interment receptacle, vault or other type of container. Nor do they include cemetery or crematory expenses, monument or marker or miscellaneous items such as the honorarium for the clergyman, flowers, additional transportation charges, burial clothing or newspaper notices)...

Of all funeral services selected in 1979 from funeral homes participating in the study: 2.36% were priced between $0 and $699, 6.7% between $700 and $1,099; 13.33% between $1,100 and $1,399; 22.34% between $1,400 and $1,699; 18.5% between $1,700 and $1,999; 7.85% between $2,000 and $2,299; and 6.5% over $2,300. The remaining 22.36% included funeral services for children, welfare recipients or partial services; i.e., less than a total funeral.

Is it true that funeral directors make a big profit?

The following are facts on which the reader can base his or her answer.

In 1979 the investment range of those participating in the previously referred to study was from an average of $147,641 for funeral homes which conducted less than 100 funerals that year to $641,703 for those that had more than 300 services.

The major expense item for a funeral home is salaries. Personnel, facilities and equipment must be available twenty-four hours a day to serve the public.

The following percentages reflect expenses involved in providing the average funeral in 1979: salaries (29.9%); burial merchandise available from the funeral director and cash advances made for the family by the funeral director (31.1%); building and occupancy (11.3%); supplies, services, collections and promotion (13.4%); automobile (5.7%); general expense (5%); and taxes (3.9%). This leaves a profit margin of 4.7%.

What should the basic philosophy of a funeral director be?

The philosophy of a funeral director should place the highest priority on the needs of the families which he serves. His first concern should be their mental, spiritual and physical well-being...

What about prearranging your own funeral in advance?

Funeral and burial arrangements are an important consideration and should be discussed openly and frankly. Prearranging and sometimes prefinancing a funeral is a method with which some people choose to assist their survivors after death occurs. However, there is no way of knowing beforehand exactly when, where, how and under what circumstances death will occur, and these unknown factors might alter original plans substantially.

Four things should be taken into consideration in planning a funeral in advance of need:

- Review the possible effect on survivors.

- Approach realistically the logic and economics of planning now what might not take place for many years.

- Keep in mind that the selection of a funeral director or a funeral firm as well as of burial merchandise, including an interment receptacle for use at a future indeterminable time, must, of necessity, be on a tentative basis.

- Monies paid in advance of need for funeral services and merchandise are governed by law in most states. Where there is no such law and monies are paid in advance, all funds should be placed in trust with the pre-arranger maintaining control of the account. Anyone making arrangements should be certain to have the right to terminate the contract at any time without forfeiture of any of the funds paid or earnings accrued.

Do memorial societies provide funeral services?

They do not. They have no licensed staff or facilities or equipment with which to conduct funerals. Most of the time they act as a third party between the survivors of a death and a funeral director with whom they have a contract or an

Howard C. Raether

understanding. This generally is done in advance of death. Contacting memorial societies immediately after death is often difficult because their telephones are not staffed twenty–four hours a day and some do not even have a phone.

What do these societies suggest and how might it affect those who follow their recommendations?

Memorial societies generally recommend immediate disposition of the body and a memorial service without the body present sometime thereafter. For most people, this is contrary to what has been learned about grief reaction. Death is a loss; and for the well–being of an individual and of society, it is important to acknowledge realistically the loss that has occurred and to give testimony to the life that has been lived. Some Americans, through the memorial society movement, attempt to sanitize their lives or intellectualize their emotions following a death by using euphemisms in their speech, disguising their behavior and sedating their emotions, as if to pretend that what has happened has, in fact, not occurred at all.

Are there alternatives to the traditional funeral?

Yes. Today there is no prescribed funeral rite or ritual for all persons. Funeral directors begin funeral arrangements by reviewing with the family the life and lifestyle of the deceased. Most funeral directors believe that the post–death activities, *including* the funeral, should not only recognize that a death has occurred but should give testimony to the life that has been lived. Therefore, the form or liturgy of the service, the music, its location, its participants and related factors are highly individualized and are intended to meet the needs of the bereaved, while at the same time giving dignity to the deceased.

"Duty calls are all that remain of the old-fashioned, affordable funeral... today it is the cost — not the thought — that counts."

Funeral Directors Are Impresarios

Deborah Wolters Reilly

Deborah Wolters Reilly is an assistant in the Rare Books Department of the University of Wisconsin. A freelance writer, she formerly was an assistant editor of *The Progressive* magazine. In the following viewpoint, Mrs. Reilly recalls the difference between old fashioned funerals and the full service funeral of today and warns that the bill for the modern services will "stimulate your full appreciation."

Consider the following questions while reading:
1. **According to Mrs. Reilly, why are funerals no longer held in the home of the deceased?**
2. **What are some of the services Mrs. Reilly claims a funeral director will provide "for a fee"?**

Deborah Wolters, "Death, Here Is Thy Sting," *The Progressive*, May 1978. Reprinted by permission from *The Progressive*, 408 West Gorham Street, Madison, Wisconsin 53703. Copyright © 1978, The Progressive, Inc.

When I was a child, my parents would take me along on their duty calls to the undertaker, where they would pay their last respects to ancient relatives, friends of relatives, and relatives of friends, who had passed on. (Often these last respects were also first respects, but, as Mother said, it was the thought that counted.

IT'S THE COST THAT COUNTS

A scant twenty years later, duty calls are all that remain of the old-fashioned, affordable funeral syntax. Today it is the cost — not the thought — that counts. And the cost of being counted is mounting.

It used to be that a body needed only one funeral service — and that directed by a clergyman. But undertakers, eschewing their Charonic image, have become impresarios, and today provide and preside over a host of professional services. Now, "professional" is always an expensive adjective. (In the funeral biz, it connotes a costly undergraduate degree in a competitive field of "mortuary science.") But the real syntactic coup has been the change from service to services. The inspired addition of a single letter has been the *sine qua non plus* — the without which nothing extra — of funerals.

Wilbert Incorporated of Forest Park, Illinois — "the full service funeral service company" — thoughtfully provides a directory to all the services you might otherwise never suspect you need:

First, there is the rental of the funeral home. Syntactical initiative in this area has brought the terminology almost full circle from the old days, when funerals actually were held in homes but people had no rental expenses because the homes were their own. Then undertakers — they were still undertakers — convinced the public that home parlors were onerous (not to mention odorous), and that a rented room specially designed for funerals — a "funeral parlor" — was required for any civilized (not to mention deodorized) send-off.

THE SPACIOUS FUNERAL FACILITIES

In recent years, several rooms have been added to the parlor, rooms you will — for an added price — not be permitted to do without. "The advantages made possible by the funeral home," Wilbert soothingly explains, include "spacious facilities" with "appropriate" furnishings.

By permission of Johnny Hart and Field Enterprises, Inc.

Among the spacious facilities is the casket showroom, appropriately furnished with "a complete selection" of caskets — formerly called coffins — in "a wide variety of styles and features." From this selection, says Wilbert, you will make the "appropriate" choice. ("Appropriate" is another one of those expensive adjectives. It replaces the more efficient but less costly modifier "only.")

Funeral fashion dictates that shrouds are out. But Wilbert advises not to worry if the deceased owns no "suitable" (read "appropriate") clothing, for "funeral directors do offer a line of burial garments."

You will also have to select a burial vault. On Pages 31 to 37 of the Wilbert directory — called *Facts Every Family Should*

Know — are illustrated displays of the Wilbert line. ("WILBERT brand burial vaults are chosen more often than any other brand.") At the top of the line is the "Triune," which features a sixteen-ounce copper inner lining, a Strentex outer lining, and a custom-crafted exterior. For a bit less, you may purchase the 'SST/Triune," with an inner lining of stainless steel. The "Venetian" and "Continental" models lack inner linings, but still offer the Strentex outer lining (or a subvariation, the Marbelon) and custom-crafted exteriors. At the bottom of the line is the "Monticello," a concrete box with Strentex lining — period.

Like most professionals, your funeral director has connections. For a fee, he will place the order for flowers since, Wilbert notes, "it has become customary (read "appropriate") to place a floral spray from the family on the casket." If you are not affiliated with a church, he can suggest a clergyman. (Members of the clergy have been relegated to the role of outside consultant in the funeral service known as "the tribute.")

Your funeral director can also obtain a flag for a veteran without charge from the Veterans Administration. (The flag is free, but the obtaining is a service, and therefore costs.) He can even arrange for burial plots.

THE BILL...AND HOW TO PAY IT

"Possibly not until after the funeral service," Wilbert chides, "will you fully appreciate the vast amount of detail, the numerous specialized services and the tremendous responsibility the funeral director has assumed in serving your family at this time of need..." To stimulate your full appreciation there will be a bill. Wilbert's catalogue discreetly omits specific dollar amounts but offers extensive advice on how to induce Social Security to share your appreciation as much as possible.

Although funerals have traditionally been go now, pay later affairs, cost accounting has come to the funeral business, and Wilbert includes a short section on pay-as-you-go and prepaid options. (The ancient Greeks also had a prepaid option: The dead were buried with coins on their tongues to bribe Charon into ferrying them across the river Styx. Mythic images are not always easy — or profitable — to eschew.)

I found my Wilbert directory in a suburban Wisconsin funeral home next to a coin-operated coffee pot — even the

PLUNDERING THE NEXT OF KIN

The decor, the stagehands, the supporting cast are all arranged for the most advantageous display of the deceased, without which the rest of the paraphernalia would lose its point—Hamlet without the Prince of Denmark. It is to this end that a fantastic array of costly merchandise and services is pyramided to dazzle the mourners and facilitate the plunder of the next of kin.

Jessica Mitford, *The American Way of Death.*

cost of the thought is mounting — but additional copies are available directly from WILBERT, P. O. Box 147, Forest Park, Illinois 60130.

The Wilbert directory has received the Good Housekeeping Seal of Approval.

"Society has assigned to (the funeral director) the role of standing as a target when the emotional concept of death is unleashed."

Funeral Directors Provide Necessary Services

Michigan Funeral Directors Association

The following viewpoint is taken from a brochure entitled "A Spoonful of Love, A Cup of Caring" sponsored by the Michigan Funeral Directors Association. In it, the association claims that the criticism of the funeral industry has strengthened the industry and that the funeral director provides a necessary service for the community.

Consider the following questions while reading:
1. **According to this viewpoint, what is the purpose of a funeral?**
2. **How does the author explain the psychological and emotional needs a funeral satisfies?**
3. **What are the capabilities ascribed to the funeral director?**

From an undated pamphlet "A Spoonful of Love A Cup of Caring," presented in cooperation with the Michigan Funeral Directors Association.

Old fashioned "home comfort remedies" served a purpose. A spoonful of this, a cup of that, a pinch of something else became the cure-all magic potion for whatever the ailment.

The old elixirs were a far cry from products available today at the corner drugstore. But the purpose is still the same: to cure and comfort the sick.

The funeral has changed, too. The "undertaker" in the black suit has given way to the funeral director. As peoples' needs and desires change, new services must be made available; equipment and facilities added.

PURPOSE OF THE FUNERAL

But, like the "old tyme" remedies versus modern miracle drugs, the purposes of the funeral remain the same: *caring for the dead, serving the living, and giving dignity to man.*
A funeral is still "a spoonful of love" and "a cup of caring." Just a bunch of words?

Too often people dismiss some of our personal and social customs as void of purpose. No reasons are given; no past performance records acknowledged; not even any meaningful or logical alternatives suggested.

The funeral and the funeral director have not escaped these attacks. But these criticisms have given strength to the funeral service industry because the public began giving more serious thought to some very potent and important facts:

The funeral is a service of love and caring in a society that, thankfully, places value in life and respect for the dignity of man, even after death;

The funeral is, in America, a basic religious rite with a proven record of bringing group support and comfort to bereaved families;

The funeral director, because of the type of service he provides, must be understanding and compassionate.

How are these general statements transferred into meaningful day-to-day performances?

Beyond proper disposition of the body, the funeral becomes a service for the living. Bereaved families and friends are able to share their grief with others. All are forced to accept the reality of death. And for many, the entire process is a further expression of religious faith, confirming their relationship to God.

If someone close to you dies, would you want to face the grief alone?

SUPPORTING THE BEREAVED

The funeral offers the opportunity for family, friends, neighbors and associates to gather in group support of the bereaved. This means simply getting together...and it's one of the most important psychological and emotional needs that is satisfied by the funeral. It is the community's way of letting others know that despite the loss of a loved one, they do not have to face the future alone. This is powerful medicine in today's society.

Psychologically, the funeral is healthy for the immediate family and closest friends. The activities associated with the funeral effectively illustrate for all the reality of death.

A leading psychologist says, "The most important thing about coping with death is understanding its reality, and the funeral conveys this feeling; when you stand in front of the casket you have to admit that death has occurred. You can see that the person has died, and you can talk with other mourners about how he lived." It may be sad and it may be tough to do, but psychological studies show you'll be healthier for it in the tomorrows.

We have funerals because we place value in life and we believe in the dignity of man. We don't drive a truck through the streets each day to collect the dead and then dump them somewhere, cover them up and forget them. Indeed, we hold the people in higher regard than the state; nations without this love and care for people show a measurable infringement upon the freedoms granted to the citizenry.

BASIC SERVICES OF THE FUNERAL DIRECTOR

Death is inevitable. When someone dies, something has to be done with the body.

Providing necessary facilities, staff and equipment represents the basic services of the funeral director. He also performs practical duties such as arrangements, notifications

HOW TO PREPLAN YOUR FUNERAL
QUEENS MEMORIAL SOCIETY
EXPRESSION OF MY PERSONAL WISHES
FOR PROCEDURES AT TIME OF DEATH

I wish to outline my preference regarding procedures to be followed at the time of my death, namely:

1. CLERGYMAN

That _____ (Church, Synagogue) be contacted immediately in order that my clergyman _____ may offer assistance to my family.

2. FUNERAL DIRECTOR

That _____ be asked to take care of the requested arrangements as itemized herein.

3. TREATMENT OF BODY

That my body be:

☐ buried in _____ Cemetery in _____

☐ cremated and my ashes:

    ☐ buried in _____ Cemetery in _____

    ☐ placed in a columbarium in _____ Cemetery in

    _____
               City and State

    ☐ disposed of as follows: _____

_____

☐ donated to _____ Medical School for anatomical science studies as per previous arrangements, copy of agreement in my personal files.

4. MEMORIAL OR FUNERAL SERVICE

That there be:

☐ a memorial service (without the body) at _____

_____ (specify location)

☐ a funeral service (with the body) at _____

_____

☐ a committal service: Private _____ Public _____

☐ no service of any kind

☐ other arrangements as follows _____

_____

5. MEDICAL RESEARCH AND HUMANITARIAN PURPOSES

That the following wishes be carried out, if possible:

☐ Donation of eyes to The New York Eye Bank
(form, completed in advance, and copy in my personal files)

☐ Permission for post-mortem examination (autopsy)

6. MEMORIAL DONATIONS OR FLOWERS

That there be donations, as specified, to:

☐ Memorial Fund of _____ (Church, Synagogue)
☐ Medical Research Charity _____
☐ Local or National Charity _____
☐ Other _____

That there be:

☐ flowers used at discretion of my family.
☐ no flowers.
☐ no limitations or restrictions as to flowers.

7. OTHER CHOICES OR WISHES (if applicable)

That there be:

☐ private service limited to family and close friends ☐ public service ☐ disposal of body, as soon as legally permissible, in manner indicated at Number 3 above.
  ☐ closed casket ☐ open casket
☐ no visiting hours and no display of my body ☐ visiting hours
☐ obituary notice at the time of death ☐ embalming
☐ obituary notice prior to a memorial service ☐ no obituary notice

8. I DESIRE THAT MY CASKET BE MADE OF:

☐ pine   ☐ stained hardwood   ☐ solid hardwood   ☐ light gauge metal
          ☐ heavy gauge metal

REMARKS: _____
_____
_____
_____

I have given careful thought and consideration to the above expressed wishes and have discussed them with my family. I understand that there is nothing legally binding in the above expression and that the ultimate decision is to be made by my next of kin. Nevertheless, I hope that my wishes will be fulfilled, to the extent that they concur with the wishes of my family.

_____ 19___ (Mr.)
                        (Mrs.)
                        (Miss) _____

                                number and street

                                city, state and zip code

Copies of this "Expression" may be filed with the Queens Memorial Society, as well as with next of kin, clergyman, or funeral director. Extra copies are available upon request.

The Society assumes no liability, financial or otherwise, in connection with the above instructions.

QUEENS MEMORIAL SOCIETY
Box 53, College Union
Queens College
Flushing, New York 11367

Raymond Paavo Arvio, *The Cost of Dying and What You Can Do About It.*

and various other requirements. These are vital tasks that most any business dealing in professional services performs for people.

The capabilities of the funeral director, however, extend beyond basic professional services. He is a professionally-trained person who must be capable of counseling and working with people at a very emotional time. He must form a partnership with the clergyman and any other family representative as they attend to procedures and details that require delicate planning and handling.

By profession, today's funeral director must be a compassionate and understanding individual. He participates in a number of community and organization activities. Funeral service is not the field for a person without these characteristics. In addition he must have a basic knowledge of psychology and human relations.

The funeral director provides necessary services for the community. But, because of the nature of these services, our society has assigned to him the role of standing as a target when the emotional concept of death is unleashed.

A leading authority on grief, who is a psycho-therapist, says that one of the important functions of the funeral director is his standing as the focal point for the death anxieties that need to be released.

In reality, the community assigns to the funeral director one of the most difficult of tasks — that of ministering to people who are faced with the fact of death. The pride that a funeral director gets from his services comes when people are helped through their times of personal crises. That's why the funeral services he provides are all about love and caring.

MY OBITUARY

The purpose of this activity is to help each student see himself or herself more objectively by reacting to his or her death.

Instructions

STEP 1. Each student should write their own obituary, imagining that you died yesterday. You may use your own format, however, you may find it easier to respond to the suggestions below.

STEP 2. When everyone has finished, volunteers may present their obituaries to the class.

STEP 3. Repeat the process, imagining that each student's death will occur five years in the future.

Suggested Obituary Outline:

Jane Doe, Age 17, died yesterday from ...

She is survived by ...

Her church membership was ...

Other organizations she belonged to are ...

At the time of her death, she was involved in ...

At her request, services will be held at ...

Donations may be sent to her favorite charity ...

She will be remembered for ...

She will be mourned by ...

Her lifetime ambitions were ...

The world will miss her because of ...

BIBLIOGRAPHY

The following list of periodical articles deals with the subject matter of this chapter.

Changing Times	*Planning a Funeral at a Fair Price*, September, 1980, p. 31.
Vincent Coppola and Mary Lord	*Regulating Death*, **Newsweek**, July 3, 1978, p. 59.
Consumer Reports	*Memorial–Society Alternatives*, August, 1979, p. 490.
William Flanagan	*In Death Be Not Proud*, **New York**, June 14, 1976, p. 75.
Good Housekeeping	*What You Should Know About Funerals*, November, 1977, p. 268.
Leon Howell	*Who's In Charge? The Church, the FTC and the Funeral Industry*, **Christianity and Crisis**, August 21, 1978, p. 195.
Human Behavior	*The Evolving Embalmer*, April, 1975, p. 52.
Roslyn Katz	*Preplanning Funerals: A Pastor's Initiative*, **Christianity Today**, January 25, 1980, p. 30.
J.J. Kilpatrick	*Big Government's Needless Interventions: FTC Regulation of the Funeral Industry*, **Nations Business**, January, 1977, p. 37.
J. Mitford	*Bake and Shake*, **New York**, January 21, 1980, p. 50.
J. Mitford	*Funeral Salesmen*, **McCalls**, November, 1977, p. 190.
Fritzie Pantoga	*A Down-to-Earth Guide to Catholic Burial*, **U.S. Catholic**, November, 1977, p. 16.
W.E. Phipps	*Consuming Fire for Corpses*, **The Christian Century**, March 4, 1981, p. 221.
U.S. News & World Report	*Should Funeral Homes Be Regulated? Pro and Con Interview With Jessica Mitford and Howard C. Raether*, May 10, 1976, p. 45.

APPENDIX OF ORGANIZATIONS

The editor has compiled the following list of organizations which are concerned with various aspects of the problems of death discussed in this book.

Abortion Education and Referral Service
3255 Hennepin Avenue
Minneapolis, MN 55408
(612) 825-4147

Primarily a public education group, the service, founded in 1971, refers those with unplanned pregnancies to the proper professional persons and/or organizations. It also provides educational materials on abortion, birth control and related subjects to students, teachers and professionals.

American Association of Suicidology
2459 South Ash
Denver, CO 80222

Founded in 1967, the association of medical and psychological professionals, social workers and clergy seeks to recognize and encourage the study of suicide, suicide prevention and related phenomena of self-destruction. The association publishes a quarterly magazine and newsletter as well as a directory of current suicide prevention centers.

American Citizens Concerned for Life, Inc.
6127 Excelsior Boulevard
Minneapolis, MN 55416
(612) 925-4395

This organization of individuals, founded in 1973, is engaged in educational, legislative, research and service activities directed toward increasing respect, protection and support for human life. The organization publishes *Update*, a quarterly newsletter, plus special reports, educational manuals and tapes.

Americans Against Abortion
6555 S.W. Lewis
Tulsa, OK 74102
(918) 494-6611

Founded in 1972, the organization is affiliated with Christian Crusade and campaigns against abortion, supporting adoption as an alternative. The organization provides speakers for radio and television and publishes booklets.

Center for Death Education and Research
1167 Social Science Building
University of Minnesota
267 19th Avenue S.
Minneapolis, MN 55455

The pioneering program in death education, founded in 1969, sponsors original research into grief and bereavement as well as studies of attitudes and responses to death and dying. The center conducts television, newspaper, college and university classes and workshops for the care-giving professions. A list of published materials and a description of the center's Cassette Tape Program is available upon request.

Concern for Dying
250 W. 57th Street
New York, NY 10019
(212) 246-6962

The organization, founded in 1967, promotes research and educational programs on prevention of "the futile prolongation of the dying process." The organization distributes the "Living Will", educational materials and films. They publish a quarterly newsletter as well as reports, brochures and bibliographies on euthanasia.

Continental Association of Funeral and Memorial Societies
1828 L Street N.W.
Washington, D.C. 20036
(202) 293-4821

The objectives of the association, founded in 1963, include promoting the dignity, simplicity and spiritual values of funeral and memorial services and reducing the costs of funeral and burial services. They promote preplanning of funerals, inform the public on funeral costs and lobby for reform of state funeral regulations. They publish the *Manual of Death Education and Simple Burial,* a bi-monthly bulletin and a handbook for funeral and memorial societies.

Cremation Association of North America
15300 Ventura Boulevard, Suite 305
Sherman Oaks, CA 91403
(213) 990-5966

Founded in 1913, the association of crematories maintains a speakers bureau and biographical archives, conducts research and compiles statistics concerning cremation. They publish the quarterly *Cremationist* and an annual directory.

Foundation of Thanatology
630 West 168th Street
New York, NY 10032
(212) 694-4173

This organization of health, theology, psychology and social science professionals is devoted to scientific and humanist inquiries into death, loss, grief and bereavement. The foundation, founded in 1967, coordinates professional, educational and research programs concerned with mortality and grief. They publish annual directories and *Thanatology Abstracts* plus the quarterly *Advances in Thanatology* and *Archives of the Foundation of Thanatology.*

International Association for Suicide Prevention
c/o Charlotte P. Ross
Suicide Prevention and Crisis Center
1811 Trousdale Drive
Burlingame, CA 94010
(415) 877-5604

Founded in 1965, the association disseminates information about suicide prevention, arranges specialized training of persons in suicide prevention and carries out research programs. The association publishes a quarterly newsletter.

174

National Abortion Federation
110 East 59th Street
New York, NY 10022
(212) 688-8516

Founded in 1977, this national professional forum for all abortion service providers acts as a clearing house for information on the variety and quality of services offered. The federation publishes *Guidlines on How to Choose an Abortion Facility* and an annual membership directory.

National Abortion Rights Action League
825 15th Street N.W.
Washington, D.C. 20005
(202) 347-7774

The organization, founded in 1969, initiates and coordinates political, social and legal action to maintain the right to legal abortion for all women. They conduct research and maintain a speakers bureau. Besides pamphlets and monographs, the league publishes a newsletter 10 times a year.

National Funeral Directors Association
135 W. Wells Street
Milwaukee, WI 53203
(414) 276-2500

The federation, founded in 1882, maintains a library of books and films on subjects related to dying, death and bereavement. Besides publications directed to members, the federation publishes an annual statistical abstract of funeral service facts and figures.

National Right to Life Committee
National Press Building
529 14th Street N.W., 341
Washington, D.C. 20045
(202) 628-4396

The purpose of this anti-abortion organization is to have Congress pass a human life amendment. The organization publishes a monthly newsletter.

National Save-A-Life League
815 Second Avenue   Suite 409
New York, NY 10017
(212) 736-6191

An organization of professionals and trained volunteers, founded in 1906, to work toward the prevention of suicide and to counsel families of suicide victims. The organization maintains a crisis center, provides a speakers bureau, sponsors educational radio programs on suicide and offers financial aid and referrals.

Planned Parenthood Federation of America
810 Seventh Avenue
New York, NY 10019
(212) 541-7800

A family planning organization, founded in 1921, with educational, research and training interests. The local affiliates provide information, medical services, counseling and referrals for contraception, abortion, voluntary sterilization and infertility services. The federation operates over 700 centers in major cities in the U.S. They publish *Washington Memo*, books, pamphlets, newsletters and an *Affiliate Directory*.

Religious Coalition for Abortion Rights
100 Maryland Avenue N.E.
Washington, D.C. 20002
(202) 543-7032

The coalition of religious organizations coordinates support for safeguarding the legal option of abortion and opposes efforts to deny this right through constitutional amendment or federal or state legislation. The organization publishes a monthly newsletter as well as pamphlets and booklets.

Society for the Right to Die
250 West 57th Street
New York, NY 10019
(212) 246-6973

Founded in 1938, the society is engaged in legislative activity and provides information on "right to die" legislation. The society publishes an annual *Death With Dignity Legislative Manual* as well as a newsletter.

Value of Life Committee
637 Cambridge Street
Brighton, MA 02135
(617) 787-4400

Founded in 1970, the committee members attempt to foster respect for life by educating and informing the public on all issues concerning life from fertilization to natural death. They maintain a speakers bureau, a library of medical and legal volumes and a newspaper file concerning abortion, euthanasia, ethics and genetics.

Index

MEET THE EDITOR

David L. Bender is a history graduate from the University of Minnesota. He also has an M.A. in government from St. Mary's University in San Antonio, Texas. He has taught social problems at the high school level for several years. He is the general editor of the Opposing Viewpoints Series and has authored most of the titles in the series.